POLICY AND PRACTICE IN HEALTH AND SOCIAL CARE
NUMBER NINE

Youth Justice

POLICY AND PRACTICE IN HEALTH AND SOCIAL CARE

POLICY AND PRACTICE IN HEALTH AND SOCIAL CARE

SERIES EDITORS

JOYCE CAVAYE and **ALISON PETCH**

Youth Justice

Edited by

Jenny Johnstone

Lecturer in Law, University of Newcastle-upon-Tyne

and

Professor Michele Burman

Co-Director, The Scottish Centre for Crime and Justice Research

Published by
Dunedin Academic Press Ltd
Hudson House
8 Albany Street
Edinburgh EH1 3QB
Scotland

ISBN: 978-1-903765-91-3
ISSN 1750-1407

British Library Cataloguing in Publication data
A catalogue record for this book is available from the British Library

Typeset by Makar Publishing Production, Edinburgh
Printed in the United Kingdom by Cpod, Trowbridge, Wiltshire
Printed on paper from sustainable resources

Mixed Sources
Product group from well-managed
forests and other controlled sources
www.fsc.org Cert no. TT-COC-2082
© 1996 Forest Stewardship Council

Contents

Series Editors' Introduction

By labelling young people as 'neds', encouraging the banning of 'hoodies' and highlighting the use of ASBOs, intensive media attention and contemporary political pressure has encouraged the demonisation of young people. The truth behind the headlines is, however, that there has been a decrease in youth crime rates, and young people rarely cause serious harm. Nonetheless, the ensuing moral panic is very influential in shaping policy devised to respond to offenders and to young people at risk of offending.

Policy and practice in youth justice in Scotland has a history of ambiguity, conflict and contradiction. These are the consequences of a system that seeks to pursue the divergent goals of justice and welfare. Welfarism is concerned with vulnerability and protection and focuses on meeting needs and on rehabilitation. These goals are in direct conflict, inevitably, with a notion of justice that implies a commitment to due process of law and individual rights. Thus problems of control and order remain at the centre of youth justice discourse and result in compromise and contradiction in terms of policy and practice.

Drawing on a range of official sources and empirical data, this critical review explores the extent and nature of offending behaviour and examines the effectiveness of youth justice policy and crime prevention programmes. The authors outline how a concern about anti-social behaviour and persistent offending has shaped the political agenda. This has led to the introduction of increasingly punitive and contradictory policy responses. They question the extent to which these changes can be said to be fully 'evidence-based'.

This book moves behind the policy rhetoric to recognise and explore some of the tensions in current policy. As such it is a valuable resource to support those working in or studying youth justice.

Dr Joyce Cavaye
Faculty of Health and Social Care, The Open University in Scotland, Edinburgh

Professor Alison Petch
Director, **research in practice for adults***, Dartington Hall Trust, Totnes, Devon*

Editors and Contributors

Susan Batchelor is a Lecturer in Criminology in the Department of Sociology, Anthropology and Applied Social Sciences at the University of Glasgow. Research interests include gender and social control, violence and social harm, youth crime and female offenders.

Michele Burman is Professor of Criminology at the University of Glasgow and Co-Director of the Scottish Centre for Crime and Justice. Her research interests include youth crime, youth justice, young female offenders, and gender, crime and justice.

Jenny Johnstone is a Lecturer in Law at the University of Newcastle Upon Tyne. Her current research interests include youth justice, restorative justice, victims and witnesses in criminal proceedings, and equality, crime and justice.

Fergus McNeill is Professor of Criminology and Social Work at the Glasgow School of Social Work and in the Scottish Centre for Crime and Justice Research at the University of Glasgow. His interests include sentencing, community sanctions, prisoner resettlement, youth justice and desistance from crime.

Mike Nellis is Professor of Criminal and Community Justice, Glasgow School of Social Work, University of Strathclyde. His research interests include community justice, penal reform and the electronic monitoring of offenders.

Kevin Pilkington is a Lecturer in Social Work at the Glasgow School of Social Work, University of Strathclyde. His research interests include youth justice, children looked after and accommodated, and the parents of looked after and accommodated children.

Susan Wiltshire is an honorary Research and Public Interest Fellow at the University of Strathclyde. Her research interests include neo-liberalism and criminal justice, the medicalisation of behaviour, religiously motivated and hate crimes, and surveillance.

Glossary of Terms and Abbreviations

Acceptable Behaviour Contract: A written agreement between a person who has been involved in anti-social behaviour and one or more agencies whose role it is to prevent further anti-social behaviour (e.g. a housing association, local authority, police or school), in which the person agrees not to carry out behaviours which have been defined as anti-social. The contracts are primarily aimed at young people but can also be used for adults and may be used with parents in relation to the behaviour of their children.

Anti-Social Behaviour (ASB): A term that covers any intimidating or threatening activity that scares the victim or damages their quality of life.

Anti-Social Behaviour Order (ASBO): A civil order granted by a court that prohibits the defendant from doing anything described in the order; an ASBO can involve criminal sanction for non-compliance.

Children's Hearing System (CHS): Part of the legal and welfare system in Scotland, the Children's Hearing System aims to combine justice and welfare for children and young people. The Children's Hearing System is comprised of regionally based welfare tribunals comprised of lay 'panels' of trained volunteers drawn from the local community which engage all parties, including the child and the child's family, in reaching a decision as to whether compulsory supervision, education and/or training are required. The overall task of the Hearing is to decide whether or not to order compulsory measures of supervision for a child and, if so, whether any conditions should be attached. A Children's Hearing is an administrative tribunal, not a court of law, and thus does not decide whether the child is 'guilty' of the offence; indeed, if there is a dispute over the facts, the case is referred to court.

Children's Panel (CHS): Part of the Children's Hearing System in Scotland. A Children's Panel is a lay tribunal made up of three trained volunteers from the community who consider the case and decide what measures of supervision, if any, are in the best interests of the child.

Children's Reporter: An official of the Children's Hearing System (usually qualified in law or social work). All children and young people who may need compulsory measures of supervision must be referred to the Reporter. The main sources of referrals are the police and social work, but other agencies such as health or education can make a referral, as well as any member of the public or even the child him/herself. When the Reporter gets a referral, s/he must make an initial investigation before deciding what action, if any, is necessary in the child's best interests. The Reporter must consider whether there is sufficient evidence to support the grounds for referral and then decide whether compulsory measures of supervision are needed. If the Reporter considers such measures are needed for the child, s/he has a statutory duty to arrange a Children's Hearing.

Community Reparation Order: An order for those aged 12 and over who are convicted of an offence involving anti-social behaviour. The order requires the person to work between 10 and 100 hours to give something back to the community they have damaged.

Community Safety Partnership: Multi-agency responses to tackling crime and disorder including anti-social and other behaviour adversely affecting the local environment as well as the misuse of drugs in their area. Statutory agencies form these partnerships and work with other local organisations and agencies.

Community Service Order (CSO): A court order requiring an offender to carry out a number of hours of unpaid work for the benefit of the community. The number of hours is decided by the court.

Intensive Support and Monitoring Service (ISMS): ISMS is a new type of disposal within the Children's Hearings System that involves monitoring by means of an electronic tag for a set period of time. This must be accompanied by intensive support during the young person's assessment for ISMS, as well as during the monitoring phase and for a period after the tagging has ended.

Ned: A derogatory term for 'a young working-class male who dresses in casual sports clothes'. However, the current stereotype is of a young person, of either sex, who engages in vandalism, petty crime, underage drinking and general anti-social behaviour.

Parenting Order: Parenting Orders can be given by the court to the parents/ carers of young people (in England and Wales and in Scotland) who offend, truant or who have received an order such as an ASBO. It normally requires the parent/carer to attend counselling or guidance for a specified period; it may also have certain conditions imposed, e.g. ensuring the child is at home at certain times, or does not visit a particular place unsupervised.

Procurator Fiscal: A Scottish public prosecutor.

Restorative Justice: A theory and a model of criminal justice that focuses on the crime as an act against another individual or community rather than the state, increasingly used in relation to young offenders. Restorative justice can take many forms but is essentially a model that builds on restitution and community participation in an attempt to engage the young person, those who are harmed, and their affected communities in deciding the response to a particular offence.

Restorative Justice Conference: A restorative justice conference aims to balance the needs of the victim and the young offender by providing a forum for discussion between the young person who has offended, the victim and all those affected by the crime. Collectively they will try to agree how to deal with the aftermath of the offence and its implications for the future.

Restriction of Liberty Order: An order imposed on those aged 12 and over requiring the offender to be in a specified place or, if more appropriate, not to be in a specified place, for a stipulated period of time.

Risk Management Authority (RMA): A statutory body created by the Criminal Justice (Scotland) Act 2003. The overall aim of the RMA is to ensure effective assessment, management and minimisation of risk of serious harm presented by violent and sexual offenders, and to become a national centre for expert advice on offender risk assessment and management.

Safeguarder: An independent person appointed by the Children's Hearings Panel or a Sheriff in certain court proceedings. Their role is to prepare a report to assist the Hearing in reaching a decision in the child's best interests.

Scottish Children's Reporter Association (SCRA): The Scottish Children's Reporter Administration (SCRA) is a national body focused on children most at risk. SCRA is at the centre of the Children's Hearings System – the child protection and youth justice system for children in Scotland. SCRA was formed under the Local Government (Scotland) Act 1994 and became fully operational on 1 April 1996. Its main responsibilities as set out in the Act are to facilitate the work of Children's Reporters, to deploy and manage staff to carry out that work, and to provide suitable accommodation for Children's Hearings.

Scottish Court Service (SCS): An agency of the Scottish Government that provides people, buildings and technology to support the operation of the courts and the Office of the Public Guardian.

Scottish Crime and Victimisation Survey (SCVS): A national victimisation survey carried out by the Scottish Government to ask individuals about their experiences of crime, and their perceptions of crime and of policing.

Secure Accommodation: A secure residential placement where young people aged between 13 and 18 years who are in care or accommodated by social services can be placed in secure accommodation. Secure accommodation is generally provided for children and young people who pose a significant risk to either themselves and/or others and are likely to run away or abscond. There are set criteria that need to be met before a child or young person can be placed in secure care: (i) they have a history of absconding and are likely to abscond from other types of accommodation and (ii) if they abscond they are likely to suffer significant harm or are likely to injure themselves and/or others. Even though these criteria may be met only a Children's Hearing or order of the court can determine whether a child or young person is detained or placed in secure accommodation.

Structured Deferred Sentence: Available only in the Youth Court. A Sheriff may defer sentence for a period of time to allow the offender to demonstrate that s/he has changed their behaviour. A 'structured' deferred sentence means that the young offender agrees to participate in particular programmes. After the successful completion of these programmes, the offender returns to court and the expectation is that s/he will be admonished.

Young Offender Institution (YOI): A secure facility accommodating 15- to 20-year-olds who have been given a custodial sentence or remanded into custody by the courts.

Youth Court: A relatively new initiative dealing with 16- to 17-year-olds, with flexibility to deal with 15-year-olds in certain circumstances. The Youth Court is a section of the Sheriff Court with designated sheriffs who have oversight of individual offenders. It has the ability to fast track cases to ensure that alleged offenders appear in court within 10 days of apprehension.

Introduction

Michele Burman

This book has two central aims: to provide a descriptive overview of current youth justice policies and practices in Scotland, and to consider the effectiveness of youth justice policy and practice within a contemporary criminal justice landscape that is characterised by much change and expansion.

For some time, there has been considerable political and public debate on crime, justice and punishment in Scotland and, within this, a particular focus on offending behaviour by young people. While the debate on the problems posed by youth offending has in many ways mirrored some of the concerns expressed in England and Wales, the work taken forward to address youth offending has accelerated and expanded greatly since devolution. All the time this has been accompanied by intensive media attention from Scotland's press given to 'the problem of youth crime' linked to what has, regrettably, become labelled as 'ned culture'. Yet, and importantly, this heightened profile given to the problem of youth crime has occurred at a time when there has been an overall drop in youth crime rates in Scotland, as in other UK jurisdictions.

Following devolution, and the establishment of a political forum and legislature in the form of the Scottish Parliament with its Justice Department and Justice Committees, matters of crime and criminal justice have been fixed even more firmly on the Scottish political agenda. In the early years following devolution virtually all aspects of criminal justice were subject to scrutiny in the form of consultation and review, resulting in an intense period of policy, legislative and governance changes affecting the provision of both adult and youth criminal justice (see Croall, 2006; McAra, 2006; McIvor and McNeill, 2007). Political activity has been accompanied by a new stress on managerialist practices in adult and youth criminal justice, with the vigorous introduction of targets and efficiency measures in the governance of crime, and the restructuring of the delivery of criminal justice services. There has also been a strong emphasis on bottom-up policy development and the mobilisation of multi-agency, area-based responses to crime. At the same time, as in other UK jurisdictions, there is also a heightened recognition of the harm done to individuals and communities by offending behaviour, and a drive towards ensuring public protection and building public confidence in both the adult and youth justice systems. There has also been an increased focus on early and targeted intervention for at-risk children and their families (see McAra, 2006). This is coupled with an increasing reliance on need–risk assessment in relation to those at risk of re-offending, and the development of mechanisms for the identification and management of risk, alongside the introduction of the Risk Management Authority.

There are two distinct processes in Scotland for dealing with young people who have been charged with an offence, although a young offender may be considered by both, depending on age or the severity of the offence. In general, however, those under the age of 16 who are alleged to have offended are referred to the Reporter for the Children's Panel and dealt with through the Children's Hearings System. Those aged over 16 are generally reported to the Procurator Fiscal and dealt with through the adult criminal justice system. The context and operational procedures of the two systems are quite different, such that the transition between them can pose particular challenges, both for offenders and for professionals.

Despite the wide-ranging differences in principles and structures across the UK jurisdictions, it has been argued that there is increasingly a similar set of demands and pressures on those responsible for the formulation and delivery of youth justice throughout the UK as a result of converging themes. As noted by Bottoms and Dignan there can be little doubt that devolution introduced turbulence into the Scottish youth justice system (Bottoms and Dignan, 2004:1) There has been a flow of new policies, interventions and initiatives, signalling youth crime and disorder as prominent political issues. Youth crime was one of the issues under consideration at the first cabinet meeting of the Scottish Executive held in 1999, at which the government announced its commitment to review youth justice. It set up an Advisory Group on Youth Crime to assess the extent and effectiveness of options available to the Children's Hearings System and the criminal courts in dealing with persistent young offenders. Their Report, published in mid-2000, identified responses to 14- to 18-year-old offenders as requiring most attention (Scottish Executive, 2000a), and put forward recommendations for a strategic multi-agency approach that would seek to balance the needs of the 16- and 17-year-old offender with public concern over the need to address offending behaviour, particularly for what was understood to be a relatively small number of persistent offenders responsible for a significant amount of offending. However, these recommendations were never fully implemented, as Scotland embarked on a more punitive course and introduced several 'get tough' initiatives. Since 2002, when the UN Committee on the Rights of the Child commented favourably on Scotland's approach to youth justice (apart from the low age (8 years) of criminal responsibility), the public debate about youth offending has been accompanied by various government plans and strategies, a number of which have been aimed at enhancing the effectiveness of the youth justice system.

The Scottish Executive produced *Scotland's Action Programme to Reduce Youth Crime* in early 2002 (Scottish Executive, 2002b). This took forward a key recommendation of the Executive's earlier review of youth crime (Scottish Executive, 2000a), namely that 'what works' principles should be incorporated into an expanded range of services, programmes and interventions for persistent offenders, and that all of these would be accessible to the Hearings System and the criminal prosecution services alike (Scottish Executive 2000a, para. 19). The importation of the 'what works' paradigm has led to a government emphasis on evidence-based policy and practice, investment in research and evaluation, and the promotion of accredited programmes for offenders (McAra, 2006; Burman *et al.*, 2006).

Scotland's Action Programme to Reduce Youth Crime included a Ten Point Action Plan on Youth Crime (Scottish Executive, 2002c) that heralded a raft of new initiatives, including Fast Track Hearings for those under 16, the pilot Youth Court for persistent offenders aged 16 to 17 years, the promotion of parental responsibility, consideration of a system of police cautions/warnings, and a review of the scope for imposing Anti-social Behaviour Orders, Community Service Orders and Restriction of Liberty Orders on persistent young offenders, all of which were subsequently introduced.

The Action Plan also included the development of a strategic framework of national objectives and standards, aimed at improving the quality of the youth justice process and services for children and young people in Scotland. *National Standards for Scotland's Youth Justice Services* was published in late 2002 (Scottish Executive, 2002a) and arranged under six objectives: to improve the quality of the youth justice process; to improve the range and availability of programmes to stop offending; to reduce the time taken from initial report to implementation of a Hearing decision; to improve the information provided to victims and local communities; to ensure secure accommodation is used when appropriate; and to improve the strategic direction and co-ordination of youth justice services by local youth justice strategy teams.

There has been a major overhaul of both the organisation and management of youth justice in recent years signalling, at the level of rhetoric and of reality, increased managerialism in the sector. Multi-agency area-based youth justice teams, involving representatives from the police, social work, health services, the voluntary sector, and the Children's Reporter, are now involved in strategic planning and the expansion of services for young offenders. Local youth justice strategy groups are charged with the development of effective preventative approaches by police, social work departments, schools, and health professionals to avoid the need for children and young people to attend a Children's Panel, and to more closely integrate the youth justice system and local authority service planning for vulnerable children. Yet the multi-agency nature of the delivery of youth justice, whether through the Children's Hearings or the adult justice system, presents a set of challenges in terms of ensuring the overall process operates effectively. Not only is there potential for inconsistency in policies and practices within the statutory agencies, which deliver services on a local basis, but the impact of these differences may be compounded when agencies with different remits, objectives and cultures come together for service delivery.

Despite longstanding differences in terms of both the underlying philosophical principles and the overarching structures of youth justice in Scotland as compared to England and Wales, there are strong concerns that youth justice policies, in particular, are becoming increasingly convergent with those found south of the border. In this context, McAra (2004; 2008) has argued convincingly that Scotland's longstanding adherence to penal-welfarism in both its adult and youth justice systems has been steadily eroded in recent years and that, particularly since devolution, this has been replaced with a more punitive criminal justice agenda. The chapters in this book try to assess the extent to which Scotland might be said to retain a distinctive youth justice culture, albeit one which, over recent years, has assumed some of the characteristics associated with less welfare-oriented jurisdictions. By way of introduction, Chapter 1 describes the overarching structures, processes and practices that characterise the current Scottish youth justice system. It outlines the legal framework within which youth justice is dispensed, and sets out the key legislative and policy developments in that regard. Currently, Scotland has one of the lowest ages (8 years) of criminal responsibility in Europe. The law as it currently stands allows children from the age of 8 to 16 years to be prosecuted in the criminal justice system, although no child can be prosecuted without the explicit guidance of the Lord Advocate, whose policy is not to prosecute children where it can be avoided. The age of criminal responsibility is considered by many to be too low and contrary to international principles and standards. The chapter discusses the benchmarks for practice set by international agreements and regulations, including the European Convention on Human Rights (ECHR) and the UN Convention on the Rights of the Child (UNCRC), and assesses the extent to which Scotland adheres to international principles.

In the face of increasing political and media attention towards the 'problem of youth crime', all UK jurisdictions are concerned with reducing youth offending, and the provision of an effective response to children and young people who offend. While Scotland's financial investment in tackling youth crime has undoubtedly increased considerably, especially since devolution, successive reports by Audit Scotland have questioned whether increases in resources have been used effectively. Several chapters in this book highlight the key challenges that are faced in the development of effective youth justice policies and practice in Scotland. Effective youth justice is essential for improving the quality of life in those communities that are adversely affected by offending and also, importantly, for improving the life chances of those young people who offend. Yet the development and adoption of effective and appropriate responses remain elusive. Asquith and Docherty (1999) noted a decade ago that there have been at least three recurrent themes in the search for appropriate and effective strategies for dealing with children and young people who offend in Scotland. The first is what they characterise as the 'pendulum-like' swing between a welfare-based philosophy and a more punitive, correctionalist approach that places greater emphasis on individual responsibility, due process and punishment (Asquith and Docherty, 1999, p. 243).

The history of youth justice in Scotland has been characterised by debates around the appropriate treatment of young offenders, the terms of which focus on the uneasy tension between the welfare needs of the individual young offender, on the one hand, and what might be conceived of as broader societal or public interest concerns on the other. Indeed the tension between the need to attend to the needs of the child while also maintaining a public interest perspective was a key factor precipitating the review of juvenile justice carried out by the Kilbrandon Committee in the 1960s (Kilbrandon Report, 1964). Charged with finding solutions to the rise in the rate of juvenile delinquency in post-war Scotland, the Committee found that most cases coming before the juvenile courts were on offence rather than care grounds, and most offences were trivial in nature. In a major departure from the adjudication and punishment model of youth justice prevailing at the time, Kilbrandon proposed an integrative welfare-oriented approach, recommending a single system of civil jurisdiction for children brought before the courts for offending, for those beyond parental control and for those in need of care and protection. No book on Scotland's youth justice would be complete without a discussion of the principles and practices of the paradigmatic Children's Hearings System, introduced by the Social Work (Scotland) Act 1968, and a direct result of Kilbrandon's deliberations. Chapter 2 describes the development of the System, founded on the key principle that welfare should be the *paramount* concern in decision making about children whether they are involved in offending or in need of care and protection, and that the welfare principle be the key test guiding decisions concerning the necessity and extent of compulsory intervention.

For almost thirty years, Scotland stood in marked contrast to other jurisdictions in its commitment to a distinctive Kilbrandon-informed penal-welfarist ethos in its youth justice system. Yet throughout this period institutional responses to offending by children and young people have segued between welfare and public interest concerns, with the latter perhaps most evident in the retention by the Crown of the right to prosecute those children who commit more serious offences in the adult criminal justice system. The Children (Scotland) Act 1995 provided a new statutory framework for the Hearings System, and introduced some important qualifications to the *paramountcy* principle, whereby the principle of public protection could be placed above that of the child's interests where the child represented a significant risk to the public. Public safety can therefore take priority over the best interests of the child. Chapter 2 argues that, since the mid-1990s, the core welfarist principles of the Hearings System have been severely tested, to the degree that there are undeniable challenges in retaining the early Kilbrandon philosophy given contemporary political pressures and the introduction of a more distinctively correctional agenda that combines an emphasis on individual responsibility and personal (and parental) accountability. Currently there are concerns that the Kilbrandon philosophy of focusing on the young person's *needs* is being overwritten by a focus on their *deeds*.

Chapter 3 draws on a range of official data sources and research material to present what is known about the extent and nature of offending behaviour by young people in Scotland. This chapter shows that youth crime rates are generally falling, in line with other European countries, and considers the contradiction that therefore seems to be exposed between youth offending rates and criminal justice policies in Scotland.

A second recurrent theme identified by Asquith and Docherty (1999) concerns the introduction of youth justice policies and practices that owe more to political ideology than systematic and rigorous research-based evidence (Asquith and Docherty, 1999, p. 244). Currently, youth justice discourse in Scotland is undoubtedly framed within a discourse of 'evidence-based' policy (Muncie and Goldson, 2006). Scotland has devoted significant resources to early intervention initiatives for 'at risk' children and their families, as well as to specialist programmes aimed at reducing re-offending among persistent offenders. Chapter 4 updates and expands upon the argument put forward by Asquith and Docherty by offering a critical account of some of the recent key developments in Scottish 'evidence-based' youth justice policy. The chapter draws on the available research evidence base in a discussion of the impact of contemporary youth justice policy initiatives, and questions the extent to which Scotland's approach can be said to be fully 'evidence-based'.

Over the past decade, Scotland has increasingly witnessed a shift towards community and diversionary strategies stemming in part from a need to address rising rates of imprisonment. Scotland is the only UK jurisdiction that routinely deals with young people aged 16 and 17 years in adult criminal courts, and in 2007/8 there were over 9,000 convictions of young men in this age group (Scottish Government, 2009a). Chapter 5 develops themes raised in other chapters by discussing the outcomes of youth justice processes, although with particular reference to the emergence of a range of community sanctions for young offenders. The chapter reviews recent statistical and research data regarding the imposition of community and custodial disposals for young people, and identifies some of the key tensions for the operation and ethos of the Children's Hearings System.

A third recurrent theme identified by Asquith and Docherty (1999) in Scotland's search for appropriate strategies for dealing with children and young people who offend is the failure, despite the commitment given in Kilbrandon, to fully and systematically implement an early preventative approach in reducing numbers of children at risk of offending in later life (Asquith and Docherty, 1999, p. 243). Now, as then, policy officials and politicians claim to be pursuing preventative, rather than retributive, goals in relation to both adult and youth justice and, within this discourse, maintain a recognition of the importance of effective early intervention strategies.

In Scotland, as in England and Wales, there has been the political perception that anti-social behaviour by young people should be as much a focus of intervention as offending behaviour, resulting in the introduction of the deeply contentious Antisocial Behaviour etc (Scotland) Act 2004, under which Anti-social Behaviour Orders were introduced for 12- to 15-year-olds. At the same time, there have also been developments in the surveillance and management of young offenders, the introduction of facilities for intensive supervision and, perhaps most controversially, the introduction and use of electronic 'tagging' for under-16-year-olds. Such developments in Scotland must surely be viewed within a context in which a gradual elision has taken place between the community safety and youth justice agendas, once more marking a shift from a more individual child-centred focus to a broader societal focus on the concerns of communities.

Courts can now impose a Restriction of Liberty Order that involves tagging the young person to enforce an order essentially restricting them to, or away from, certain locations at particular times. Children's Hearings Systems also have the power to impose conditions restricting the movement of a young person where he or she meets the criteria for secure accommodation. In addition to monitoring, any young person subject to a 'tag' also receives a combination package of both monitoring and support, known as an Intensive Support and Monitoring Service (ISMS). Although the government claims that the ISMS is designed with the welfare needs of the child in mind, it is hard not to see this and other similar developments as signalling yet another shift from the welfarist concerns and ethos of minimal intervention espoused by Kilbrandon. Of crucial significance here is that these measures are being implemented in a context of falling crime rates, and in which convictions for young offenders under 21 years are decreasing and offence referrals to the Children's Hearings System are relatively stable.

Parenting Orders are another anti-social behaviour measure introduced by the 2004 Act in Scotland. These orders are based on the assumption that certain parents either deliberately disregard, or are incapable of addressing, the needs or behaviour of their children, and that compulsory measures are required to ensure that their parenting is of an acceptable standard. The emergence and the impact of the anti-social behaviour agenda in Scotland, and the spirited resistance against this agenda on the part of social workers and civil liberty groups, is discussed in more detail in Chapter 6. Although the number of orders imposed on young people in Scotland has so far been low, anti-social behaviour discourse and practice have created tensions with approaches to dealing with young offenders through the Children's Hearings System. Audit Scotland (2007) established that most councils have found it difficult, both strategically and operationally, to overcome the differences between the child-centred focus of the Children's Hearings System and the community-focused design of the legislation (Audit Scotland, 2007, p. 18). Anti-social behaviour strategies also have the clear potential for alienating the communities they seek to serve, not least the young people residing within them.

The final chapter provides a summary of the main themes addressed in the book, and considers future directions within a youth justice system that is increasingly subject to managerialist imperatives and incentives. The provision of services to young offenders is delivered within the context of the Concordat between central and local government. Yet the focus on service provision as the vehicle for delivery of outcomes has implications not only for effective multi-agency working but also for the impact on the young person. While the potential of the Scottish system is great, it remains unfulfilled. The future of the Children's Hearings System is unclear: its core principles appear untenable and some of the formal disposals of the System have become progressively more punitive. There are numerous structural (and resource-based) difficulties that create barriers to diversion, leading in turn to greater criminalisation and prosecution of young people. The growing punitive approach taken towards young offenders in Scotland, with its emphasis on the 'toughening–up' of sanctions, risk assessment and surveillance, risks eroding the very important distinction between youth justice and adult criminal justice in Scotland that Kilbrandon so strongly underscored. The adoption of a risk-based agenda for youth justice presents many practical and ideological challenges for those who work within it. Along with an emphasis on the identification and management of risk posed by young people, Scotland has also witnessed increased emphasis on the responsibilisation of individual young people, their parents and, as evidenced by a recent Government publication on youth offending (Scottish Government, 2008g), the community within which the young person resides. Youth justice in Scotland is indeed in a period of turbulence.

CHAPTER 1

Youth Crime and Justice: Law and Process

Jenny Johnstone

Introduction

This chapter examines Scots law and process relating to youth crime and justice. It discusses the terminology used within the youth justice process and looks at future changes. In Scotland, the Children's Hearing System is the primary youth justice agency, dealing with both young offenders and victims, and those subject to care proceedings. As discussed in the next chapter, Scotland recognised very early on that a separate system was required for young people. One significant recent development, however, has been the piloting of the Youth Court, which poses some challenges to both the ethos and practice of the Hearing System.

Figure 1.1 shows the youth justice process in Scotland and its relationship with both the adult and the Youth Courts. The process, changes and challenges facing the Hearing System are discussed in more detail in Chapter 2, including the key elements of the initial referrals, the acceptance of the grounds of referral, the Hearing itself, decision as to outcome and custody and care issues. This chapter examines some concerns around process, legal challenges that the Hearing System has faced and, in particular, the relationship with the Youth Court.

Referrals come from many different sources, including police, social work, education, nurseries and youth clubs, and for a variety of reasons, including truanting, glue sniffing, neglect and running away. Applying Packer's model of due process (Packer, 1968), the requirement to make the implications for the

Figure 1.1 Flowchart of the youth justice process

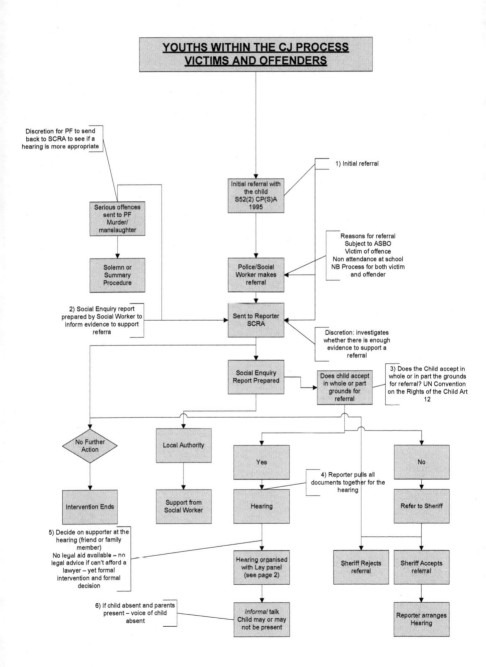

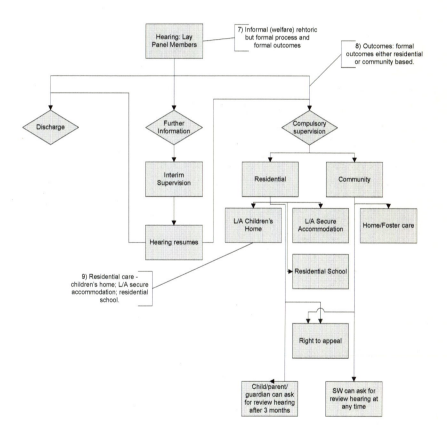

Hearing: Lay Panel Members

7) Informal (welfare) rehtoric but formal process and formal outcomes

8) Outcomes: formal outcomes either residential or community based.

Discharge

Further Information

Compulsory supervision

Interim Supervision

Residential

Community

L/A Children's Home

L/A Secure Accommodation

Home/Foster care

Hearing resumes

9) Residential care - children's home; L/A secure accommodation; residential school.

Residential School

Right to appeal

Child/parent/ guardian can ask for review hearing after 3 months

SW can ask for review hearing at any time

grounds of referral clear to the child can be seen as a due process safeguard. A Safeguarding Officer can be appointed and now representation and legal aid can be provided to represent the child in situations where the child is present or absent. The case of *S* v. *Miller* in 2001 highlighted the case for legal aid to be made available for young people who are required to appear before a Children's Hearings Panel after concerns under Article 6 of the European Convention of Human Rights were raised regarding the right to a fair trial. While the Children's Hearings Panel is not a court it is still deemed to be a legal tribunal and as such will make decisions that are legally binding and enforceable. It should therefore be recognised as a very formal rather than informal process, although Panel members might like to see it as formal informalism.

The notion that tribunals represent the informal legal process is potentially misleading. Genn (1993), for example, recognises the formal rules and procedures by which these tribunals have to abide and notes that the outcome can be very formal and bring with it sanctions for non-compliance. The lay Panel can also provide a misleading representation of informalism. Formal Panel Member training now places more emphasis on the knowledge and practical application of the legal requirements. The recent change in process whereby the Reporter enters the Hearing room at the same time as the families and young people means Panel Members' awareness and knowledge of the structure is of crucial importance. The legislative changes that have recently been proposed have met with a wary response from current Panel Members.

As discussed in Chapter 2, lay Panel members are volunteers working in a public sector setting and have a responsibility to understand the rules of procedure and the emphasis on working in the best interests of the child, especially in understanding the circumstances of the case and the young person and ensuring the outcome meets the needs of the individual child. One of the gaps in terms of research is understanding how these decisions are reached, justified and communicated to the young person and how the welfare approach is evidenced in the outcome of the proceedings. Do we know to what extent the young person fully understands the nature of the Hearing, the outcomes and the impact of what they communicate within the Hearing itself? And can we say that this is a formal intervention process requiring due process safeguards for those who are made subjects of it? The rhetoric surrounding the System does suggest a more informal rather than formal *legal* process but the outcomes that can result, for example the loss of liberty, suggest the opposite.

A significant development has been the piloting of the Youth Courts in the early part of this decade. In England and Wales under the Criminal Justice

Act 1991 Youth Courts were set up to deal with 10- to 17-year-olds. In 2002 the Scottish Executive's 10-point Action Plan contained the commitment to look at the feasibility of establishing a Youth Court to tackle 16- to 17-year-old persistent young offenders. The December 2002 recommendation of the Feasibility Group (see Chapter 4) was that a Youth Court would be possible under existing Scottish law, and the group proposed a model to be located within Hamilton Sheriff Court. In June 2003 the Hamilton Youth Court was established with four permanent Sheriff Court judges presiding over youth court cases only, on a twice-weekly basis. The Youth Court targets the 16- to 17-year-old age group with flexibility to deal with 15-year-olds in certain circumstances. It has three distinctive features. First, it focuses on young people within the criminal justice system and designates sheriffs to work specifically with them. Second, a fast-track process is used to deal with the young offenders to ensure that they come to court quickly. In the majority of cases alleged offenders are making their first appearance in the Youth Court within ten days of the date the crime was committed, commensurate with the commitment under Article 40 of the United Nations Convention on the Rights of the Child. Third, designated sheriffs share the work in the Youth Court and provide consistent supervision of every young offender who comes to the court, overseeing their progress in meeting the sentence requirements. This development is in keeping with the move towards a more case-managed approach to offenders. An evaluation has shown that, as a result, the number of guilty pleas emerging from the Hamilton Youth Court is unusually high, at around 75% (McIvor *et al.*, 2006).

Domestic Law and International Obligations

The United Nations Convention on the Rights of the Child (1989) provides that every organisation dealing or working with children should act in the 'best interests of the child' (Article 3). Article 12 (2) provides that every child should be given the opportunity to be heard in any judicial or administrative proceedings affecting the child, either directly or indirectly, through a representative. Article 40 sets out some expectations of states in dealing with young people who have been accused of a crime and against whom proceedings are being brought. It also states that state parties should 'recognise the right of every child alleged as, accused of, or recognized as having infringed the penal law to be treated in a manner consistent with the promotion of the child's sense of dignity and worth' (UN Convention on the Rights of the Child, 1989).

Recognition of the needs of child victims is apparent in Article 39, which requires countries to promote physical and psychological recovery and reintegration of child victims. In 1989 the governments represented at the General Assembly (which included the UK) agreed to adopt the convention into international law and it came into force in September 1990. States which are party to the convention, including the UK, have to report to the Committee on the Rights of the Child. This United Nations treaty-monitoring body assesses how well states are implementing the convention, reports on progress and makes recommendations. The committee comprises 18 independent children's rights experts who are elected in their personal capacity to four-year terms. The committee, which meets three times a year in Geneva, Switzerland, is responsible for examining the progress made by state parties in fulfilling their obligations under the convention. Unlike some treaty-monitoring bodies, the committee does not have the power to examine individual complaints concerning violations of the rights of a child. While there are specific principles in place there are also general principles: that all procedures should be in the best interests of the child (Article 3) and free from discrimination (Article 2); that judicial bodies/tribunals must take into account the evolving capacities of the child (Article 5); and that they should give weight to the views of the child (Article 12).

The recognition of these articles throughout both the Children's Hearing System and the Youth Courts is critical. The introduction of the Youth Court has raised the concern that it represents a more systematic and punitive or justice-oriented approach compared to the welfare-oriented approach of the Children's Hearing System. However, a closer examination of the Children's Hearing System shows that the welfare approach can be seen more as rhetoric than reality.

The United Nations Rules for Administration for Juvenile Justice (1985, Beijing Rules), United Nations Rules for Administration of Juveniles Deprived of Their Liberty (1990), the United Nations Guidelines for the Prevention of Juvenile Delinquency (1990, Riyadh Guidelines) and the European Convention of Human Rights (Article 5, right to liberty and security and Article 6, right to a fair trial) which have been adopted by the Human Rights Act 1998 are significant but the extent to which nation states have adopted these provisions is variable.

The judgment of the Court of Session in August 2001 following the case of *S* v. *Miller* (2001) stated that:

Although the Court concluded that the Children's Hearings system as a whole complied with the requirements of the European Convention on Human Rights, it was ruled that legal aid requires to be available in circumstances where there are complex legal issues to consider, where the child may not understand the process or where there exists the possibility of deprivation of liberty. (*S v. Miller* 2001 SC 977; Scottish Council on Tribunals, 2002)

New provisions allow the Children's Hearing to appoint a legal representative from a list and the cost will be met from public funds. This strongly suggests that there is a need to ensure that the CHS has skilled and appropriate representation in place for young people appearing before it and reiterates the formal rather than informal nature of the proceedings and potential outcomes, challenging the welfare philosophy underpinning it. Due process safeguards need to be present to protect the young person.

Defining the concepts: minimum age of criminal responsibility, youth, youth crime, youth justice, and anti-social behaviour

Newburn (2002b) describes youth as an 'elastic' concept, having different meanings at different times. Different jurisdictions have different minimum ages of criminal responsibility.

The minimum age of criminal responsibility in Scotland is 8 years of age. No one under this age can be charged with a criminal offence. However, criminal proceedings may be brought against those aged 8–16 subject to strict control by the Lord Advocate's Guidance. In the case of *T* v. *UK* and *V* v. *UK* (2000) it was argued that setting the age of criminal responsibility as low as 10 breached the Human Rights Act 1998. The ECHR said that although there was no common standard among the member states as to the age of criminal responsibility and even though England and Wales had a low age, the age of 10 was not so young

> as to differ disproportionately from the age limit followed by other European states. In those legal systems recognizing the concept of the age of criminal responsibility for juveniles, the beginning of that age shall not be fixed at too low an age level bearing in mind the facts of emotional, mental and intellectual maturity. (United Nations Standard Minimum Rules for the Administration of Juvenile Justice, Rule 4.1)

The United Nations Committee recommends 14 years; however in Scotland children under the age of 8 years are deemed to be *doli incapax* (incapable of evil). As part of the philosophy underpinning the process in Scotland and in line with key international obligations, diversion from prosecution is a central principle. Where children aged over 8 and under 16 years have committed a very serious offence (such as murder), they will be referred to the Procurator Fiscal, and prosecuted before a criminal court. This could culminate in one or more of a range of court-imposed sanctions that could include detention in secure accommodation. Approximately two-thirds of young people in secure accommodation in Scotland are placed there on the authority of a Children's Hearing. The remaining third of the secure care population are subject to a criminal court order, either serving a sentence for a serious crime or on remand (Walker *et al.*, 2005). There is also a range of community-based disposals, including community service and probation, supervised attendance orders and the controversial Restriction of Liberty Orders, which involve electronic tagging.

Apart from determining legal liability for a crime, the age of an offender will also affect where and how the young person is dealt with in the youth justice system. The minimum age that an offender may be dealt with as an adult is 16 years and, unlike other parts of the UK, Scotland deals routinely with young people aged 16 and 17 in criminal justice proceedings. The Youth Court, introduced for 'persistent young offenders' aged 16 and 17 in 2003, possesses the same powers of sentencing as the adult criminal Sheriff Summary court and, therefore, adjudicates with all the legal equivalence of an adult jurisdiction. The Youth Court can impose a custodial sentence and a wide range of community-based disposals. There is also a range of 'dedicated programmes' for offenders, including offending reduction programmes, addictions services, alcohol and drug awareness, family group conferences, and restorative justice services. These are provided by a variety of agencies through local authority social work departments.

The recent Criminal Justice and Licensing (Scotland) Bill can be seen as an attempt to demonstrate adherence to international principles and standards and to bring Scots law more into line with jurisdictions across Europe. The Bill proposes the introduction of the restriction on prosecution of children under 12 years. By so doing, it implements the main recommendations of the Scottish Law Commission's *Report on Age of Criminal Responsibility* (2002). In essence, the Bill proposes that 8 years would be retained as the age below which children are deemed incapable of committing crime, 12 would be introduced as the age below which children are immune to prosecution and 16 would remain as the (usual) age of automatic referral to the adult justice system. Another way of reading the Criminal Justice and Licensing (Scotland) Bill might be to suggest that there may be grounds here for arguing that the debate about raising the age of criminal responsibility is evidence of a re-assertion of welfarist values.

The Crime and Disorder Act 1998 defines anti-social behaviour as 'Behaviour which caused or is likely to cause, harassment, alarm or distress to one or more persons not of the same household' (CDA 1998 s19 (1)). Anti-social behaviour can give rise to an Anti-social Behaviour Order (ASBO). As discussed in Chapter 6, an ASBO is a civil order which can involve criminal sanction for non-compliance. While these orders target what could be seen as the risk factors they do not tackle the root causes: good behaviour cannot be imposed by coercive measures. However there are some welfare elements behind this development, for example early intervention and addressing the risk factors of criminal behaviour.

Models of youth justice

It has been accepted in many jurisdictions for some time that special procedures are needed to deal with young offenders, and a series of different philosophies have developed reflecting conflicting views on how young offenders should be dealt with. There are two main approaches predominant in the youth justice debate – justice and welfare. Systems of youth justice have been based on balancing, on the one hand, the need to punish or control young offenders and encourage them to take responsibility for their actions (justice) with, on the other hand, the need for strategies that take account of the many problems that may lead to involvement in crime (welfare). While the over-riding principle of working in the 'best interests' of the child and key international obligations provide for a welfare-oriented approach, the application of the law can give rise to a conflict.

The justice model includes the following elements:

- adherence to a fixed procedure;
- a formal approach with legal processes involving representation;
- presence of an adversarial approach with the defence and prosecution battling it out in the court room;
- a formal setting where everyone clearly has their role and responsibility;
- punishment proportionate to the offence committed;

- young persons deemed to be made responsible and culpable or blameworthy for an offence when they have reached a certain age (age 8 in Scotland);
- emphasis on the act in question rather than the actor (consider the impact of the new rules on disclosure).

These elements are evident in the adult and youth justice processes in Scotland.

The welfare model, on the other hand, provides for a more adaptable procedure with the following elements:

- a multi-agency intervention or holistic response to discussing possibilities in dealing with the offender's behaviour;
- a minimalist approach with the Hearing preferring resolution-finding rather than conflict within the process (inquisitorial approach);
- a more informal process which involves the young person in forming the outcome;
- addressing the offender's needs and meeting the needs of the young person in any outcome; giving priority to the reasons why the offender committed the crime and responding to these rather than determining culpability;
- emphasising the individual rather than the act.

Restorative justice approaches, it has been argued, fall into this latter category.

If we take the components of these various models and apply them to the practice of youth justice in Scotland we can see that there has been an attempt within the process to combine welfare and justice principles. However, academics (for example, Fionda, 2005; Muncie *et al.*, 2002) suggest that these two paradigms produce conflict and tension among those given responsibility for developing youth justice policy. In Scotland, in recent years, there has been an expansion in policy and practice for dealing with young offenders, including attempts at different sentencing options as well recognising the need for more diversionary strategies. Some of these practices are underpinned by welfare principles but operate in such a way as to extend the widening of social control measures. For example, ASBOs, contracts and curfew orders are examples of civil orders against children which ultimately can result in a criminal sanction if they are breached.

In the Report of the Advisory Group on Youth Crime (Scottish Executive, 2000a), it was suggested that the Children's Hearing is not understood by the public, and is not living up to the principles laid down in the welfare approach.

Commentators on the Hearings system (McIvor, Hallett) explode the myth that the Hearings System is well understood by the people of Scotland. Not only is it not well understood, it is quite often misunderstood. It is very much a closed system: no information is released about children who appear at Hearings, press reporting is curtailed and Hearings are held in private. Although this is quite proper in terms of the privacy of the individual children whose cases are considered by Hearings, it leaves victims and members of the community with few places to raise questions, record complaints or contribute positively. In the cases of children who persistently offend, there may be many victims affected by the actions of one child, and many of these victims may be children themselves. Identifying a role for members of the community, including victims, is a major challenge to the Hearings system and should be further considered. Voluntary reparation schemes could play a positive part here. (see www.scotland.gov.uk/youth/crimereview/summary.asp)

As stated earlier in this chapter, the Lord Advocate, in issuing prosecution guidelines to divert as many 16- and 17-year-old offenders as appropriate to the Hearings System, instructs Procurators Fiscal to take full account of public interest and public safety in all such cases. The Advisory Group on Youth Crime maintains that young people can be assisted in making a successful transition into adulthood if the system sets out to divert as many as possible of those involved in minor offences out of the system altogether, and delay as long as possible the entry of more persistent offenders into the adult system. The Group refers to the 'repertoire of services' that makes available to young people a range of 'accredited programmes and interventions', from which should be developed a package that meets the 'needs and deeds' of each young person. The starting point of each programme would be a risk assessment and would contain an element of challenging offending behaviour. *Getting It Right for Children and Young People who Present a Risk of Serious Harm* (Scottish Government, 2008e) has been published as a working document to guide practitioners and service deliverers in managing the risk of serious harm. Practitioners can use the documents and templates to provide evidence that they have the appropriate processes and staff in place to meet the young person's needs and to reduce risks for the community, staff and child or young person and their family. For young people especially responses to offending behaviour are generally multi-agency responses requiring the appropriate staff to be in existence across agencies. These protocols and risk assessments must be shared, acknowledged and adhered to, and this requires an acceptance and understanding on the part of all the staff involved. However, as Burman *et al.* (2007) note, joined-up working is 'often dictated by the strength of personal relationships, which can often be insufficiently robust to withstand the power of competing organisational goals' (www.rmascotland.gov.uk/ViewFile.aspx?id=328). They suggest that joint training on these initiatives is required to address conflicts between these competing organisational goals and provide a coherent response to the young person concerned.

Pervasiveness, Early Intervention Strategies and Risk

The Scottish Executive's *Review of Youth Crime: Preventing and Responding to Criminal Behaviour by Children and Young People* (1997) summarises the relevant risk factors that academics have suggested predispose young people to offending behaviour. The Report suggests that there is a striking consensus about this and how to deal with offending behaviour:

> that the risk factors are multiple and detectable early in a child's life; that the earlier risk factors are addressed the better; that risk factors for youth offending can be addressed as part of wider programmes to improve the life circumstances and life chances of the children at risk; that exclusion – from home, school, community – tends to exacerbate, not address, risk factors and finally that locking up older children who have embarked on a pattern of offending behaviour is unlikely to break the pattern. For most young offenders whose crimes do not fall into the 'serious' category, non-custodial disposals are far more likely to be more effective and more cost effective. (Scottish Executive, 1997)

The extent to which early intervention and risk strategies have permeated the social justice mechanisms – prior to offenders entering the criminal justice process – can be seen as an attempt to widen the net of social control, or as an attempt to address these predisposing/risk factors in order to provide a more holistic and welfare-oriented approach. Enrolling young people in sports programmes is one method of attempting to ameliorate crime and anti-social behaviour. Many of these programmes tend to focus on diversionary and rehabilitative approaches. There is evidence that the programmes alone do not reduce offending but they do bring benefits in terms of personal and social development for the young people involved (Ruiz, 2004). Nichols (2007, p. 204) argues that 'in the context of programmes to reduce youth crime, sport is a tool to facilitate a process, much more than an end in its own right, and needs to be used with sensitivity'. It can be a challenge to provide the resources to offer such programmes to young people, and their effectiveness needs to be evaluated and monitored and potentially accredited in order to ensure consistency and quality. Successful programmes need to focus on offending behaviour (including specific types of offending, such as car crime) and be underpinned by the principles of effective practice. They should also promote social inclusion by addressing issues related to offending, such as physical and mental health, substance misuse, education and training, employability, family and relationships, accommodation, and use of leisure. Another key element is the implementation of restorative approaches being used in many jurisdictions including Scotland. Currently used specifically for young offenders, these approaches seek to involve victims more directly in the process of tackling offending behaviour.

In conclusion, the system, or process, as it currently operates provides examples of considerable tension between the predominant models of youth justice – the welfare and justice approaches. The recent recommendations for reform to the Children's Hearing System through the Criminal Justice and Licensing Bill coupled with the proposal to raise the age of criminal responsibility to 12 in Scotland may show a commitment from Scotland to align itself with international obligations in recognising the rights of the child but its implementation may represent a more punitive approach. The formal mechanisms of disposal that the Children's Hearing System allows will become more streamlined under the proposed changes, making it a more formally recognised tribunal. The discretion in decision making is evident and in order to fully understand how our youth justice process operates we need to review how Panel members make their decisions and how criminal justice agencies are responding and making decisions to divert or prosecute young people.

CHAPTER 2

The Children's Hearing System

Susan Batchelor and Michele Burman

Introduction

The Social Work (Scotland) Act 1968, implemented in 1971, introduced a distinctive approach to dealing with the problems of children and young people in Scotland. Following the recommendations of the Kilbrandon Committee, which reported in 1964, juvenile courts were replaced by Children's Hearings which deal with both children in need and children who offend. These welfarist principles have pertained for 30 years, and are now incorporated in the Children (Scotland) Act 1995. However, post-devolution the system has experienced some challenges: for example the introduction of Anti-social Behaviour Orders (ASBOs), Restriction of Liberty Orders (RLOs), and electronic monitoring for young offenders, as well as the piloting of Fast Track Hearings for persistent young offenders and specialist Youth Courts. In addition, the system now faces an ever-increasing proportion of children referred on care and protection as opposed to offence grounds. This chapter presents an overview of the Children's Hearing System, tracing its history and underlying philosophy, as well as discussing recent challenges.

History and Philosophy of Kilbrandon

In May 1961, the Secretary of State set up a committee, chaired by Lord Kilbrandon (a High Court judge), 'to consider the provisions of the law of Scotland relating to the treatment of juvenile delinquents and juveniles in need of care or protection or beyond parental control and, in particular, the constitution, powers and procedures of courts dealing with such juveniles' (Kilbrandon

Committee, 1964/1995, p. 5). The Kilbrandon Committee contained in its membership a chief constable, a headmaster, a Scots law professor, a child psychiatrist, a chief inspector of child care and probation, two sheriffs, and two justices of the peace. Yet despite its apparently traditional membership the Committee put forward a radical and far-reaching set of recommendations that profoundly affected the way in which children and young people were dealt with in Scotland (Burman *et al.*, 2006, 2007; Lockyer and Stone, 1998b).

The Committee began with the assumption that children and young people appearing before the juvenile court – be it as a result of offending, truancy, being outwith parental control, or lack of parental care – showed similar underlying difficulties and had a common need for special measures of education and training. For this reason, they claimed, a 'legal distinction between juvenile offenders and children in need of care or protection was ... of little practical significance' (Kilbrandon Committee, 1964/1995, p. 8). Delinquency was described as 'a symptom of personal or environmental difficulties' (p. 8) which could be traced to 'short-comings in the normal "bringing up" process – in the home, in the family environment and in the schools' (p. 32). Kilbrandon deemed the existing juvenile courts ill-equipped to deal with these difficulties and recommended that, with the exception of those charged with exceptionally serious offences, all children and young people up to the age of 16 years in need of 'compulsory measures of care' should be brought before a new and specialised treatment agency or juvenile Panel. The underlying principles of such a Panel were to include:

- separation of the judgement of evidence from the disposition of a case;
- community involvement in the form of lay participation in decision making;
- adoption of a preventive and educational approach;
- involvement of parents in any measures to treat children.

Thus, the traditional role of the court as an arena of adjudication and punishment was to be replaced by lay tribunals which, as a result of their non-adversarial and relatively informal setting, would engage all parties, including the child and his or her family, in reaching a decision as to whether compulsory supervision, education and/or training were required (Lockyer and Stone, 1998b). The overall and paramount principle was to be that children and young people should be treated according to their 'needs not deeds' (McDiarmid, 2005). In other words, compulsory measures could only be justified when they were in the 'best interests' of the child.

As Lockyer and Stone (1998b, p. 11) acknowledge, while this proposal undoubtedly reassured both the public and the Scottish legal profession, 'it created a certain inconsistency in the argument that the offence was not a reliable indicator of the seriousness or complexity of the child's overall situation'. As we shall see below, this twin-track approach has been the subject of some criticism.

While the shift from courts towards a system based on social education was generally welcomed at the time, some criticised the Committee's recommendations as being 'too soft' (Fox, 1991; Kearney, 1998). Despite these criticisms, the subsequent White Paper, *Social Work and the Community* (SED/SHHD, 1966), accepted the majority of the Kilbrandon Committee's proposals with one important exception. The White Paper proposed that new generically structured social work departments, rather than the 'social education departments' envisaged by Kilbrandon, should provide reports and supervision duties for the Children's Hearings (Martin and Murray, 1976; Stone, 1995). The White Paper proposals were enacted in the Social Work (Scotland) Act 1968 and the new social work departments came into being on 17 November 1969. The Children's Hearings System commenced operations on 15 April 1971 and remained largely unchanged until the Children (Scotland) Act 1995.

Review and reform

While it was not without its critics, Scotland's unique system of dealing with youth justice and child protection was both a source of national pride (Morris and McIsaac, 1978) and international interest (Fox, 1991). Initially Hearings were concerned mainly with children referred on offence grounds, but in the late 1970s reported incidents of child abuse increased and in the 1980s child sexual abuse began to be acknowledged as a widespread problem. The system also had to adapt to the extensive social changes that took place in relation to family life during this period, particularly increases in single-parent and step-parent family structures, drug addiction, alcohol abuse and domestic violence (Stone, 1995). A major concern became the provision of adequate services for children and families in the light of growing demands on limited resources.

In the late 1980s and the early 1990s, a number of high profile cases brought the public's attention to some of the difficulties of the system, in terms of its resourcing and capabilities, while the passing of the UN Convention on the Rights of the Child gave children's needs a higher political profile.

The 1989 UN Convention on the Rights of the Child, which was ratified in the UK in 1991, addresses the spectrum of the rights and needs of children and young people up to the age of 18 years. Like the Children's Hearings System, it looks at the whole child, and includes within its ambit concerns about the care and protection of children as well as offending behaviour. There are a number of relevant articles under the Convention that resonate clearly with the aims and principle of the Hearings System: Article 1, which defines children as all those under the age of 18; Article 3, which states the *best interests* of the child must be at least a primary consideration in actions concerning children, including courts of law; Article 37, which requires strict control of any deprivation of a *child's liberty*; Article 40, which acknowledges the reality of offending behaviour by children, sets out standards for dealing with this (including the right to privacy), directs states to set up *procedures* for dealing with child offenders that are specifically geared towards them, encourages diversion from the courts so long as human rights and legal safeguards are respected, and gives examples of a variety of welfare and educational *disposals* appropriate to the well-being of children and proportionate to individual circumstances.

The UN Convention on the Rights of the Child is monitored by the United Nations Committee on the Rights of the Child. Following its scrutiny of the UK's second report to the Committee (2002), it expressly welcomed the approach to youth offending taken by the Children's Hearing System, and also welcomed the debate on the inclusion of 16- to 18-year-olds within the ambit of the Hearings, while also expressing concern that children could be tried in adult courts. The Committee expressed strong concern at the low age of criminal responsibility in Scotland, and recommended that it be raised significantly. It also recommended that appropriate resources should be allocated for the Children's Hearings in Scotland to allow the number of cases dealt with to be substantially increased and to allow young offenders of 16 to 18 years of age to be included in the Children's Hearings system.

The framing of key elements of juvenile justice in terms of welfare values was a relatively stable feature of Scottish policy for over a quarter of a century. Following devolution however, Scotland has seen a steady flow of new policies, legislative changes and initiatives relating to youth justice, together with an overt political commitment to a more punitive approach to youth offending (Burman *et al.*, 2006; McAra, 2006). In recent years, policy has shifted from a concern with the social and personal needs of young offenders to a focus on the nature and frequency of their offences. There is now an increased emphasis on investigation, risk assessment and surveillance. These developments have been taken to signal a convergence of youth justice policy with New Labour in England and Wales (see, for example, McAra, 2004; 2006) and form the broader context within which developments in Scottish youth justice need to be understood. In June 2002 the Scottish Executive launched a 10 Point Action Plan to reduce youth crime which included the piloting of specialist Children's Hearings and Youth Courts to fast track persistent young offenders (discussed in more detail in Chapter 4), Antisocial Behaviour Orders for 12- to 15-year-olds (discussed in Chapter 6) and other developments flowing from the 10 Point Action Plan. There have been a number of policy initiatives aimed at enhancing the effectiveness of the system, including the implementation of national objectives and standards, and the creation of multi-agency youth justice strategy groups (which have a key role to play in the planning and development of services).

Post-devolution, the number of referrals continues to grow. There has been continuing – and increasing – difficulty in recruiting lay Panel members, and growing problems in finding social work staff to provide services for children. A review of the Children's Hearings System in 2004–5 sought to ask fundamental questions about the operation of the system, devised 30 years before, as a result of significant changes in workload. The review raised concerns that this might lead Scotland to shift far away from the welfare-based approach that had characterised it for so long.

These wider developments in youth justice since devolution have placed increased pressure on the Kilbrandon principles and the Hearings model in terms of youth justice policies for dealing with offending by young people through the Hearings System. In all this there remains the tension between the 'correctional drift' seen elsewhere in the UK and the welfarism of the distinctive Children's Hearings approach to youth justice of which Scotland is proud.

THE STRUCTURE OF THE SYSTEM

Scottish Children's Reporter Administration (SCRA)

The decision to refer a child to a Hearing is the responsibility of the Reporter, an independent official (usually qualified in law or social work) whose principal task is to investigate cases in order to establish whether there is sufficient evidence to support the statutory grounds of referral and, if so, whether compulsory measures are required to help address the needs and/or behaviour of the child. Reporters are also involved in arranging review hearings, warrant hearings, and other related maters. Akin to the Procurator Fiscal in the adult criminal courts, Reporters have considerable discretion and are often referred to as the 'linchpin' of the Panel system (Thomson, 1991). When the Hearings System was initially established, there was a separate Reporter's department in each of the 12 regional and island authorities across Scotland. In 1994, however, Reporters were brought together to become one national body under the Local Government etc (Scotland) Act. The Scottish Children's Reporter Administration (SCRA) became fully operational on 1 April 1996.

Children's Panels

Decisions at the Hearings stage are made by three members of the local children's Panel. Scottish Ministers are required to appoint a Children's Panel for each local authority, with a chairperson and deputy chair. There are currently around 2,800 Panel members across Scotland, ranging from approximately 659 in Glasgow to 17 in Shetland (SEED, 2007). All are unpaid volunteers, drawn from the local authority area, who receive initial and in-service training. The initial period of appointment is three years and is renewable following monitoring of performance and attendance at training. Panel members sit on Hearings on a rota basis and make decisions as to whether children are in need of compulsory measures of supervision.

Children's Panel Advisory Committee (CPAC)

Each local authority is required to appoint a Children's Panel Advisory Committee (CPAC). There are currently 30 CPACs operating in Scotland — one for each local authority but with a joint CPAC for Clackmannanshire, Falkirk and Stirling (SEED, 2004). CPACs are usually made up of around three volunteer members appointed by Scottish Ministers and two members nominated by the local authority (usually local councillors). The responsibilities of CPACs include: recruiting new Panel members, monitoring the performance of existing members at Hearings, assessing Panel members for re-appointment, and advising Scottish Ministers on certain matters relating to the general administration of Panels (e.g. the number of members to be appointed to the Panel, or the extent to which further training may be required) (SEED, 2004).

The Hearings process: the referral

Referrals to the Children's Hearings System are made to Reporters, independent officials who are located in each local authority area. Children can be referred from birth until age 15 on care and protection grounds and from age 8 until age 15 on offence grounds (8 being the age of criminal responsibility). They can be retained in the system until age 18 through the extension of existing supervision requirements. Most offenders aged 16–17 are dealt with in the adult system, but a Sheriff can remit such cases to a Hearing for advice and/or disposal. In practice, however, only very small numbers are ever remitted (McAra, 1998). As recommended by Kilbrandon, the Crown reserves the right to prosecute under-16-year-olds in the adult criminal courts in exceptionally serious cases (e.g. homicide or rape) and also in certain specified motor vehicle offences (McAra, 2004). This amounts to what Asquith labels a 'twin track approach': 'for the majority of children, punishment and judicial proceedings are seen to be inappropriate. For the minority of serious or persistent offenders, judicial intervention and punitive measures may be imposed' (Asquith, 1996, p. 11).

Although anyone can refer a child or young person to the children's Reporter, the majority of referrals come from five main sources: the police, social work, education, health, and parents (SCRA, 2006). The most frequent source of referrals, on both offence and non-offence grounds, is the police (McAra, 2002; McAra and McVie, 2005), who were responsible for 87% of all referrals in 2005/6 (SCRA, 2006). The grounds for referral, set out in section 52(2) of the Children (Scotland) Act 1995, are diverse and include the neglect and abuse of children, the commission of offences by children, as well as dealing with children who are 'beyond the control of a relevant person' or who fail 'to attend school regularly without reasonable excuse'. A child may be referred on more than one ground and these may include both offence and non-offence grounds. In a study conducted shortly after the inception of the system, Martin et al. (1981) revealed that almost three-quarters of children were referred to the Reporter on offence grounds. Today's figures are dramatically different, in that the majority of cases referred to the Reporter relate to non-offence grounds, as Tables 2.1 and 2.2 demonstrate.

While the number of children referred to the Reporter on offence grounds increased by 7% between 2003/4 and 2005/6, there was a 9% increase in children referred due to lack of parental care and a 34% increase in those referred because they were the victim of an offence (Table 2.2). Indeed, the numbers in the latter category have increased by a massive 308% since 1996/97 (n=4,249) to become the third most common ground for referral in 2005/06 (n=17,331). In the same year, the number of children referred to the Reporter due to lack of parental care exceeded the number referred on offence grounds for the first time (SCRA, 2006, p. 30).

Table 2.1 Children referred to the Reporter on offence and non-offence grounds, 1996/97 and 2005/6

	1996/97 Number (%)	2005/6 Number (%)
All Grounds		
Girls	9,349 (35%)	22,533 (42%)
Boys	17,513 (65%)	31,229 (58%)
Total	26,862 (100%)	53,883 (100%)
Non-Offence Grounds*		
Girls	6,961 (48%)	19,843 (48%)
Boys	7,513 (52%)	20,975 (52%)
Total	14,474 (100%)	40,818 (100%)
Offence Grounds*		
Girls	2,962 (20%)	4,222 (24%)
Boys	11,589 (80%)	13,392 (76%)
Total	14,551 (100%)	17,614 (100%)

* These figures include children who have also been referred on both grounds, offence and non-offence

Source: SCRA Annual Report 2006

Table 2.2 Grounds of referral for children referred to the Reporter, 2003/4–2005/6

Grounds for referral	Number of children referred		
	2003/4	2004/5	2005/6
(a) Beyond control of any relevant person	4,183	4,558	5,107
(b) Bad associations or moral danger	2,590	3,083	3,004
(c) Lack of parental care	16,266	16,781	17,801
(d) Victim of a Schedule 1 offence*	12,929	16,270	17,331
(e) Member of the same household as a victim of a Schedule 1 offence*	1,788	1,684	1,629
(f) Member of the same household as a Schedule 1 offender	1,022	816	876
(g) Member of the same household as an incest victim or perpetrator	23	15	36
(h) Not attending school	3,407	3,137	3,291
(i) Allegedly committed an offence	16,470	17,494	17,624
(j) Misused alcohol or drugs	1,611	1,369	1,426
(k) Misused solvents	44	29	17
(l) In the care of the local authority, and special measures are necessary	77	50	36
Total children referred**	45,793	50,529	53,883

*Any of the offences mentioned in Schedule 1 to the Criminal Procedure (Scotland) Act 1995 (offences against children to which special provisions apply, e.g. sexual offences, bodily injury, or cruelty).

**These totals count every child referred to the Reporter once for the year. A child may be referred to the Reporter more than once in the year on the same and/or different grounds.

Source: SCRA Annual Report 2006

The investigation

After receiving a referral, the Reporter carries out his or her own investigation as necessary. This involves requesting information on the child and their circumstances from relevant agencies, e.g. the local authority social work department, the child's school or nursery placement, health visitors, and so on. Having considered the available data, the Reporter may decide: (i) to take no further action; (ii) to refer the case to the local authority social work department for voluntary advice, guidance and assistance; or (iii) to arrange a Hearing. In approximately two-thirds of cases the Reporter is satisfied that alternative measures to compulsory supervision are appropriate (Scottish Executive, 2004a). For example, where a child or young person admits that they have committed an offence, the Reporter may arrange some form of reparation or refer them to another service, such as family support or mediation. Table 2.3 illustrates Reporter decisions on cases disposed of in 2005/6.

Table 2.3 Reporter decisions on children referred, 2005/6

Reporter decision	Number of children		
	Non offence	**Offence**	**Total**
Arrange children's Hearing	4,674	2,296	6,255
Custody referral to the procurator fiscal	0	230	230
Custody referral to the Reporter	0	6	6
Joint report to procurator fiscal	Less than 5	890	891
Measures already in place	4,022	2,921	5,881
Diversion to other measures	191	4,345	4,457
Family have taken action	3,021	947	3,873
Insufficient evidence to proceed	7,918	1,582	9,392
No indication of a need for compulsory measures	20,930	8,573	28,318
Refer to local authority	5,150	1445	6,035
Total*	40,287	17,755	53,223

*The totals do not equal the sums as children can be referred more than once in the year and may have multiple Reporter decisions. Reporter decision was not recorded in 37 cases.
Source: SCRA Annual Report 2006

The Hearing

Once the Reporter has referred a child to a Hearing, decision making passes to the lay tribunal of three Panel members. There must be three Panel members present at any Hearing, including a chair person and one member of each sex. The only other people with a right as well as an obligation to attend all the stages of the Hearing are the child and the relevant persons. That said, the Panel has the power to release the child from this obligation in certain circumstances. This is normally decided at a business meeting. Under the

Children (Scotland) Act 1995, 'relevant persons' refers to anyone with parental responsibilities and anyone who ordinarily has charge of the child, but excludes unmarried fathers who do not live with the child and do not legally have parental responsibilities.

Responsibility for the procedural management of the Hearing rests with the Panel chair, while the Reporter acts in a 'quasi-legal advisory role' (Finlayson, 1976), keeping a record of proceedings and alerting the chairperson to any procedural or human rights requirements that have not been adequately addressed. A social worker is also usually in attendance to provide expert advice and assessment, while others such as teachers, family representatives and safeguarders attend less frequently. A Hearing may appoint a safeguarder to offer an independent view on what is in the child's best interests. Where a case is legally complex or deprivation of the child's liberty (e.g. secure accommodation) is being considered the Hearing will appoint a legal representative to represent the child's views.

On average, Hearings last between 15 minutes and three-quarters of an hour (Asquith, 1983; Hallett *et al.*, 1998). The chairperson usually opens by introducing the Panel members and the Reporter to the child and his or her family, and then asking the child to confirm his name, date of birth, and address. He or she then goes round the table to ask each of the other participants to introduce themselves, thereby establishing their right to attend. If there are new grounds of referral to be established, these will be read out to the child and his or her family, who will have to indicate whether they accept or reject the grounds as detailed. If the grounds are disputed, or the child is too young to understand, it is open to the Panel either to discharge the case or refer it to the sheriff for proof. If the grounds are established, the case is returned to the Hearing for disposal. In 2005/6, 3,435 applications were made to the Sheriff Court, and 89% were held to be established (SCRA, 2006).

During the Hearing, Panel members hold a full and frank discussion with all participants, in order to garner as much information as possible about the child and his or her family. That said, they necessarily rely heavily on information provided in the social work report that is made available to the Panel members, the family and normally the child (if over 12 years old) prior to the Hearing. As Griffiths and Kandel (2006) acknowledge:

> Much of the information provided through conversation at the Hearings comes from participants who are, generally, not legally represented. Nor are such individuals experienced in speaking within

legal or conference settings. In such contexts, they may become vola-
tile and angry with one another or the decision makers. In addition,
the child, who is the most important individual present, is often
uncommunicative or sometimes even defiant. (Griffiths and Kandel,
2006, p. 141)

Outcomes

At the end of the discussion, each Panel member gives his or her own individual decision and the reasons for it to everyone present. The overall task of the
Hearing is to decide whether or not to order compulsory measures of supervision for a child and, if so, whether any conditions should be attached (e.g.
residence in foster care or residential accommodation, attendance at school or
a programme designed to address offending behaviour). In practice, the majority of Hearings result in a supervision requirement. In 2005/6, for example,
less than 10% of cases where the grounds were accepted or established were
discharged by Panels (SCRA, 2006). Once a supervision requirement is made
it is the statutory responsibility of the local authority social work department
to implement it. Supervision requirements normally last for one year, but may
be reviewed sooner if there is a change in circumstances or the supervision
requirement is not being complied with. Children and/or relevant persons have
the right to appeal the Hearing decision and may ask a further Hearing to
suspend the supervision requirement pending any appeal.

Research on effectiveness

Although the underlying principles of the Children Hearings System are
widely regarded in Scotland and beyond, overall there has been relatively
little independent systematic evaluation undertaken and, where this has
taken place, findings present a mixed picture.

A three-part study of the System was commissioned in the late 1990s by the
Scottish Office. The research found a lack of clarity about decision making in
the system, a fairly substantial drift in time intervals, and a failure to prevent
escalation in offending among a small group of older male offenders at high
risk of progression to the adult courts (and subsequently prison) (see Hallett
et al., 1998; Waterhouse and McGhee, 2000). The research identified failures of
implementation rather than a failure of ethos (see Murray *et al.*, 2002; Hallett
et al., 1998) and suggested that that the system was better at tackling problems
posed by children referred on care and protection grounds rather than those
posed by offenders (Hallett *et al.*, 1998). The research also indicated some

inconsistencies in Reporters' decision making (Hallett *et al.*, 1998; Waterhouse *et al.*, 2000). On a more positive note, the research found that participants consider the non-adversarial system fair and feel their views are listened to by Reporters and Panel members. Despite feeling nervous, families spoke positively about the informality and ease of communication in Hearings (Hallett *et al.*, 1998; Waterhouse *et al.*, 2000).

A later report by Audit Scotland (2002) that examined how the Children's Hearing System and the criminal justice system in Scotland deal with offenders under 21 years raised several further criticisms. The Report found a Hearings System that is under considerable strain as a result of internal and external resource problems, is subject to delay and suffers from a lack of available services. Audit Scotland's review found a lack of investment in provision and specialist staffing, with over two-thirds of resources being taken up by process costs rather than service provision for young people. Recently, Audit Scotland (2007) reported that the principles underpinning the system have been put under increased pressure due to referral activity, raising more questions about the capability of the system to deal with the demands placed upon it, as well as deeper concerns about its future.

Conclusions

Despite the uncertainty about the future of Children's Hearings, a key strength of the Scottish youth justice system is that it has thus far largely managed to avoid the more punitive approach taken in England and Wales. The System continues to be seen as a successful mechanism for taking many young people under the age of 16 out of the adult criminal justice system, with no apparent adverse effects on levels of youthful offending, which is proportionately lower than in England and Wales (Whyte, 2005). However, as stated in the earlier part of this chapter and in other chapters in this book, the dominance of welfarism within Scottish youth justice has diminished quite markedly in recent years (Burman *et al.*, 2006; McAra, 2004; McAra, 2006). Recent policy and legislative developments in youth justice have impacted on the criminal justice response to youth offending and the management of young offenders in a way that poses serious challenges to the Kilbrandon ethos.

The original Kilbrandon philosophy was to focus on 'needs' not 'deeds' of children. This served to emphasise the similarities between those children in need of care and protection and those who came to the attention of the Hearings because of their offending behaviour. The welfare of the child was paramount. The growing punitive approach taken towards young offenders in

Scotland, with its emphasis on the 'toughening-up' of sanctions, risk assessment and surveillance, risks eroding the very important distinction between youth justice and adult criminal justice in Scotland that Kilbrandon so strongly underscored.

The Scottish juvenile justice system, which enjoyed a high degree of stability from the 1970s through the mid-1990s, has undergone significant changes, and is now clearly under threat. As will be argued in other chapters in this book, recent years have witnessed a new era of juvenile justice, one that is underpinned by a complex set of rationales that tend to locate the interest of society above the interest of the child. It is hard not to conclude that policy has slowly shifted from a concern with the social and personal needs of young offenders to a focus on the nature and frequency of their offences. With an emphasis on persistent offending, the development and expansion of programmes based on 'what works' principles (focused on criminogenic needs rather than welfare-based needs) pose yet more of a challenge to the welfare-oriented and child-centred ethos of Kilbrandon.

CHAPTER 3

What's the Problem? The Nature and Extent of Youth Offending in Scotland

Michele Burman

'40% rise in violent crime by under-18s' (*The Guardian*, 16.5.2008)

'Young offender statistics to be revised as crime rate worsens' (*The Scotsman*, 12.7. 2007)

'Fall in Dundee youth offending' (*Evening Telegraph*, 11.7.2007)

'Youth crime down by half' (*Evening Times*, 22.7.2005)

'Majority of youth crime is theft-related and on rise, says Executive' (*The Scotsman*, 4.4.2005)

Introduction

In recent years, Scottish youth justice policy has undergone a shift from a concern with the social and personal needs of young offenders to a focus on the nature, extent and frequency of their offences and a concomitant emphasis on investigation, risk assessment and surveillance. Yet, despite longstanding political and media attention given to youth crime, the task of obtaining meaningful data about the nature and extent of young people's offending behaviour in Scotland is far from straightforward.

There are approximately 920,000 young people aged 8–21 years living in Scotland, accounting for about 18% of Scotland's total population of 5.1 million. How many of them are offenders? What kinds of offences are they committing? Is youth offending in Scotland unusually high? Answers to these questions are not readily available. This is, in part, an artefact of the two different systems for dealing with young people who offend in Scotland. The type of administrative data collected about offenders and offences by the different agencies involved (police, social work, Reporter) differs quite markedly and is by no means cross-referable. Gathering *comparable* and reliable information about the numbers of young people going through the Hearing System and the adult criminal justice system is problematic as some agencies count cases, not individuals (e.g. number of referrals to the Procurator Fiscal) and some young people commit more than one offence (and so can go through the system(s) more than once in any given year). The complexity of the picture of the extent of youth offending is further complicated by the relationship between reported crime and detected youth crime, and the differences between local and national data, such that a clear and robust answer to the supposedly straightforward question of whether youth crime is rising or falling is not easy to come by.

Yet censorious stories about youth and crime are a staple of the Scottish media, and youth crime rates are a fairly consistent media preoccupation. There tends to be a reliance on official statistical figures, which are in themselves problematic, as they only capture what is reported to and recorded by police, and provide only partial information. A glance at Scottish newspaper headlines in recent years will show the extent to which mixed messages are conveyed about the levels and types of offending behaviour engaged in by young people. Different interpretations are given to the same sets of figures, as the above headlines show. Little wonder that, despite strong evidence that the majority of officially recorded crime is carried out by adults, public perceptions right across Britain tend to overstate the extent of crime attributable to young people (see NACRO, 2001).

In Scotland, relatively limited systematic information has been available on public understanding and attitudes toward youth and crime until fairly recently. As part of the 2004 Scottish Social Attitudes survey, the Scottish Executive funded a module of questions aimed at exploring public attitudes towards young people, with particular reference to youth crime. The study found that 69% of respondents were of the view that the amount of crime committed by young people had increased over the past decade, and just 2% thought it was lower (Anderson *et al.*, 2005). While those in the oldest age group (65 years and over) were most likely to think youth crime was higher, such a view was almost equally common among those aged between 18 and 24 years (75% and 73%, respectively). Between a half and two-thirds of respondents also thought that each of a series of specific youth crime-related problems were either 'fairly common' or 'very common' in their own area

– groups of young people hanging around the street (67%), vandalism/graffiti (49%), problems caused by young people who have been drinking (53%), problems caused by young people who have been using drugs (35%). These findings led the researchers to comment that:

> The study reveals a widespread belief that the level of youth crime is higher than a decade ago and a view that youth crime-related problems are very common in respondents' own areas – even if such attitudes are not necessarily supported by external evidence or data on the direct effects on respondents of young people's behaviour. Overall, the survey suggests that direct experience alone cannot explain levels of public concern. (Anderson *et al.*, 2005)

Available data sources

So what data sources are available? The Scottish Government publishes official statistical bulletins on police-recorded crime, court proceedings statistics, social work and prison statistics. In addition, the Scottish Children's Reporter Administration publishes an annual report on Children's Hearings referrals and outcomes. So while there are a number of different data sources that yield information about offending and offenders, all have limitations on the extent to which they provide accurate and reliable information on crimes and offences committed by young people. A key problem when discussing crime figures, however, is that crime is not an uncontested social fact: it arises from moral judgements, a legal code, crime classification and numerous decisions taken by individuals about whether or not to invoke the legal process on a particular occasion (Smith and Young, 1999, p. 14).

Police-recorded crimes and offences

Police-recorded crime statistics present crimes and offences[1] recorded and 'cleared up' by the eight Scottish police forces (see, for example, Scottish Government, 2008i). Note that 'clear-ups' do not necessarily result in a report being made by the police to the Procurator Fiscal. Police-recorded crime statistics provide a breakdown of the number of crimes committed by crime type and by local authority area. The recorded crime statistics in Scotland (unlike in England and Wales) include both 'offences' (more minor infractions such as breach of the peace, simple assault) as well as more serious 'crimes' (such as robbery and sexual assault). While these statistics provide a measure of the volume of crime with which the police are faced, they provide only a partial picture of the actual level of crime. Not all crime is reported to the police or recorded by them, and a significant number involve no known offender. The statistics are offence- rather than incident-based; several crimes or offences may occur in the course of one criminal incident, and an offence may have more than one victim and be committed by more than one offender. Thus police-recorded statistics are not directly comparable with statistics on action taken against offenders, as one offence may lead to several persons being charged, or one offender may be charged with several offences.

Police-recorded crimes and offences (all ages) in Scotland rose steadily throughout the 1960s and into the 1990s. Following a more general pattern across Europe, the increase in Scottish crime rates in the latter decades of the twentieth century saw a gradual lessening and levelling off from the mid-1990s onwards and became relatively stable until the early years of the millennium when the statistics registered an increase. Most of this increase, from 2004 onwards, results from the impact of changes in police recording practices due the implementation of the Scottish Crime Recording Standard (SCRS), which led to the recording of more minor offences, such as vandalism and minor thefts, than previously. Overall, reported crimes (all ages) in Scotland decreased significantly from a peak of 572,921 in 1991, to 385,509 crimes in 2007/8 (Scottish Government, 2008i). The numbers of offences similarly decreased over the same period (Scottish Government, 2008h). Once the changes in policing and recording practices are taken into account, there is no real evidence of any significant increase of more minor offences. Importantly, the number of more serious violent crimes, such as serious assault and robbery, has levelled off, and there has been a marked decrease in burglary (Scottish Government, 2008i).

An important limitation of the police-recorded crime figures is that they are not routinely broken down by age (or gender), and so are limited in the information they can provide about the extent to which recorded crimes and offences are committed by young people.

Estimates of youth offending have been derived from reviews of data held by several sources. For example, a 'snapshot' review of the offender files carried out by the Scottish Criminal Records Office in March 2001 revealed over 76,000 recorded offenders under the age of 21 years (including those whose cases were still pending). According to Audit Scotland (2002, p. 10) this represents one in 12 young people in Scotland (or 8% of 18- to 21-year-olds).

Table 3.1 illustrates recent estimates provided in a report on crimes committed by young people (aged 21 and under) in Scotland (DTZ Pieda

Consulting, 2005). The report draws on a range of official data sources, including police-recorded crime statistics, and estimates that 43% of all crime is attributable to young people aged under 21 years (or in other words, most crime is committed by adults). The crimes in question are primarily public order crimes, and low-level theft: fire-raising (86%), vandalism (75%), theft of motor vehicles (75%), theft by opening lock-fast places (65%), handling offensive weapons (59%) and housebreaking (55%). The report found that young people are less likely than adults to commit crimes of indecency (41%), other crimes of dishonesty such as fraud and reset (30%) and motor vehicle offences (26%) (DTZ Pieda Consulting, 2005). Audit Scotland estimated that youth crime in relation to property offences, cost business, private individuals, and the public sector more than £80 million per year (Audit Scotland, 2002).

Table 3.1 Estimated proportion of selected crimes due to young people, 2005

Crime category	No. of recorded crimes	% of incidents due to young people	No. of recorded crime due to young people
Crimes of violence	16,461	42%	6,957
Crimes of indecency	6,552	41%	2,705
Crimes of dishonesty	235,668	54%	127,284
Fire-raising, vandalism etc	95,470	75%	71,953
Other crime	72,883	39%	28,588
All crime	427,034	56%	237,487
All offences	508,855	33%	167,243
All crimes and offences	935,889	43%	404,730

Source: Adapted from DTZ Pieda Consulting (2005) *Measurement of the Extent of Youth Crime in Scotland.*

Table 3.2 Proportion of youth crime due to specific age-groups and gender (2005)

Crime category	15 yrs and under	16–17 yrs	18–21 yrs	Males	Females
Crimes of violence	24%	20%	56%	90%	10%
Crimes of indecency	60%	14%	27%	85%	14%
Crimes of dishonesty	34%	17%	49%	85%	15%
Fire-raising, vandalism etc	65%	12%	23%	90%	10%
Other crimes	24%	16%	60%	90%	10%
All crimes and offences	36%	15%	49%	87%	13%

Source: Adapted from DTZ Pieda Consulting (2005) *Measurement of the Extent of Youth Crime in Scotland.*

Table 3.2 presents these same findings in terms of age categories and gender of the young person. In keeping with the international picture, the DTZ Pieda report estimates that the bulk of youth crime in Scotland is attributable to those aged 18–21 (49%), with those aged under 15 years disproportionately responsible for offences such as fire-raising, vandalism and indecency. The authors of the Pieda Report (2005, p. 36, para 4.38) make clear that this finding is anomalous, but do not offer any explanation. Again, in keeping with patterns elsewhere in the world, young men are overwhelmingly responsible for the majority of youth crime (87%), with a far smaller proportion attributable to young women (13%).

Criminal proceedings and convictions

The further an offender progresses in the criminal justice system, the more becomes known about him or her. The Scottish Government annual statistical bulletin *Criminal Proceedings in the Scottish Courts* provides information on the types of crimes and offences for which persons are convicted, and on sentencing outcomes, as well as information on the characteristics of convicted offenders. This includes details on age and gender, and is therefore useful in any attempt to estimate the proportion of crime committed by young people (see, for example, Scottish Government, 2008b). Though at this point in the criminal process it is possible to analyse offending by age and gender, it should be emphasised that the statistics relate to *criminal convictions*, rather than crimes. It should also be noted that an individual may be proceeded against on more than one occasion over the course of the year, with several charges involved on each occasion. Those under 21 years are more likely than older offenders to be convicted on a number of occasions and hence to be counted more than once.

In 2001, referring to youth crime data from *Criminal Proceedings in the Scottish Courts 1999*, Audit Scotland concluded that the scale of youth offending in Scotland was 'significant', with young people responsible for a high proportion of high volume crime: 'Its scale leads to a very significant effect on crime figures as a whole. The rate of offending by young people is disproportionately high compared to their number in the population' (Audit Scotland, 2001, p. 12).

But, ten years on, is this still the case? The total numbers of people (all ages) proceeded against in the courts decreased from 174,500 recorded for 1996/97 to 153,900 in 2006/7. Similarly, conviction rates in Scotland declined from the mid-1990s and then were relatively stable from the millennium onwards (Scottish Executive, 2006c). Persons with a charge proved (crimes and offences) for all age-categories decreased steadily, from 151,565 in 1996/97 to 138,830 in 2006/7 (Scottish Executive, 2006c; Scottish Government, 2008b).

Table 3.3 shows the patterns, from 1997/98 to 2006/7, of criminal convictions for those aged under 21 years. It is important to emphasise that criminal proceedings data do not include most offences referred to the Children's Hearings System.

Table 3.3 Males and females under 21 with charge proved per 1,000 population, 1997/98 to 2006/7

Type of Accused	97–8	98–9	99–00	00–01	01–2	02–3	03–4	04–5	05–6	06–7
Males Total	64	59	55	48	52	54	54	56	55	58
under 16	0.5	0.4	0.3	0.2	0.3	0.5	0.4	0.4	0.5	0.5
16 yrs	74	75	60	44	51	57	56	56	67	68
17 yrs	196	177	163	141	139	144	152	146	148	167
18 yrs	250	228	205	193	203	193	199	182	185	194
19 yrs	254	218	200	180	195	203	197	182	177	182
20 yrs	216	216	185	169	191	194	187	167	164	171
Females Total	10	9	8	8	8	9	10	10	10	10
under 16	0.06	0.01	0.02	0.04	0.02	0.02	0.07	0.07	0.03	0.05
16 yrs	7	8	6	5	5	6	5	7	8	7
17 yrs	22	21	19	16	17	17	17	17	21	22
18 yrs	28	29	26	24	22	23	21	23	24	27
19 yrs	28	25	26	23	26	24	25	23	21	25
20 yrs	27	26	26	23	22	27	25	25	21	23

Note: The figures do not reflect actual numbers, but rather refer to numbers per 1,000 population.
Source: Adapted from Scottish Government (2007a) *Criminal Proceedings in Scottish Courts, 2006/07*, Table 5

In keeping with past trends across the UK and the international picture, the data record that young males are far more likely to be convicted of an offence than females, and the proportions attributable to both genders have remained relatively constant over time. The most common age of conviction, however, varies between genders. For females, the peak age has fluctuated around the age of 20; whereas for male it is around 18 years.

Table 3.4 shows the numbers of male and females aged under 21 years with a charge proven against them. The totals listed are total convictions for the gender in question for crime or offence category. Although total male convictions (all ages) for all crime and offences have decreased significantly since the mid-1990s (from 130,961 in 1996 to 108,189 in 2005–6), convictions for under-21-year-old males have decreased still more rapidly (from 31,852 in 1996 to 24,413 in 2005–6) (Scottish Government, 2007a). A similar trend is in evidence for crimes of dishonesty over the same time period: 8,919 to 3,146 for under-21s; 23,259 to 13,781 for total convictions (Scottish Government, 2007a). Non-sexual crimes of violence have decreased at a similarly

Table 3.4 Males and females under 21 years with a charge proved, by main crime/offence, 2006/7.

Main crime or offence	Males under 21yrs		Females under 21	
	Number	**%**	**Number**	**%**
All crimes and offences	26,912	100	3,418	100
All crimes	10,980	41	1,284	38
Non-sexual crimes of violence	719	3	69	2
Crimes of indecency	131	*	13	*
Crimes of dishonesty	3,163	12	574	17
Fire-raising, vandalism	2,372	9	190	6
Other crimes	4,595	17	438	13
All offences	15,932	59	2,134	62
Miscellaneous offences	10,606	39	1,665	49
Motor vehicle offences	5,326	20	469	14

Source: Adapted from Scottish Government (2007a) *Criminal Proceedings in Scottish Courts, 2006/07*, Tables 6 a) and b).

significant rate (1,560 to 588 for under-21s; 4,019 to 1,820 for total convictions); while crimes of indecency have decreased slightly overall (546 to 542), the rate has increased slightly for under-21s (94 to 116). Convictions have not decreased in all crime or offence categories. Crimes of fire-raising and vandalism showed an increase for under-21s (1,908 to 2,078) while decreasing overall (4,796 to 4,234). Finally, 'other crimes' (predominantly drug-related crime and crimes not elsewhere classified) have also increased slightly for under-21s (3,495 to 3,866), and more substantially overall (11,707 to 14,392) (Scottish Government, 2007a).

Overall, female convictions for all crimes and offences increased notably for the first few years of the millennium before decreasing slightly, although convictions for under-21s decreased steadily. For crimes of dishonesty, though the overall rate has decreased slightly since the mid-1990s (from 4,820 in 1996 to 3,697 in 2005–6), the number attributable to under-21s has decreased more rapidly (1,046 to 549) (Scottish Government, 2007a). In both crimes of indecency and non-sexual crimes of violence, rates for under-21-year-old females and total convictions have shown similar decreases over the time-period. Both overall and for under-21-year-olds, convictions for fire-raising and vandalism, and other crimes, have increased slightly giving a slightly more mixed picture.

Declining rates

On the whole, however, and even with the well-known limitations of such data, the available Scottish statistical data sources show that offending by young people is declining. This decline in youth crime in Scotland reflects a similar decrease in crime overall, both in the UK and in many other parts of the world during the same period (see Young, 1999). In Scotland in 2005/6, an estimated total of 142,200 persons were proceeded against in court, a decrease of 5% on 2004/5, and 19% below the figure of 174,500 recorded in 1996/97 (Scottish Government, 2007a). Between 2004/5 and 2005/6, the overall number of convictions per 1,000 population decreased from 56 to 53 for males and from 10 to 9 for females. Moreover, the number of convictions per 1,000 population in 2005/6 was generally lower than it was ten years previously for younger offenders (Scottish Government, 2007a). This is not simply due to a failure in police detection rates; the most recent Scottish Crime and Victimisation Survey (2005/6) also indicates that crime victimisation levels are back to around those recorded in 1992 (Brown and Bolling, 2007).

Referrals to the Reporter

But not all crimes result in court proceedings. Court data needs to be supplemented with data from the Scottish Children's Reporter Administration in any attempt to estimate the proportion of crime committed by young people. As described in Chapter 2, when the alleged offender is a child, a referral will normally be made to the Reporter to the Children's Panel, and a high proportion of offences committed by young people are dealt with by the Hearings System. The Scottish Children's Reporter's Administration provides a summary and analysis of data on numbers of young people referred to the Hearings System on offence grounds, therefore providing information on incident rates. As documented in Chapter 2, SCRA data show a gradual increase in the total numbers referred to the Reporter, although the increase is largely due to numbers referred on non-offence grounds, whereas the numbers referred on offence grounds have remained relatively constant over the past ten years. To put this into some context, there are just under 600,000 children between the ages of 8 and 16 years in Scotland. Of the 56,199 children referred to the Children's Reporter in 2006/7, 16,490 were referred on offence grounds and 44,629 were referred on care and protection grounds. Where there is some gender parity in relation to numbers of referrals on care and protection grounds, males are far more likely than females to be referred on offence grounds, as Table 3.5 shows. That young men constitute the greater proportion of overall offence referrals is not surprising given that gender is a strong predictor of offending.

Table 3.5 Numbers of boys and girls referred to Reporter on offence and non-offence grounds, 2006/7.

Grounds for Referral	Number	%
All Grounds		
Girls	24,263	43
Boys	31,891	57
Total	56,199	100
Non-Offence		
Girls	21,900	49
Boys	22,690	51
Total	44,629	100
Offence Grounds		
Girls	4,032	24
Boys	12,452	76
Total	16,490	100

Source: Adapted from SCRA (2007) *Annual Report, 2006/07*, Table 2.

'Persistent' Young Offenders

For most young people, their offending behaviour is 'transitory' and linked to their social development (Jamieson *et al.*, 1999). As discussed later in this chapter, self-report studies, which ask respondents to talk about how many offences they have been involved in, if any, in the preceding year (or over the course of their lives) confirm that minor offending during the teen years is fairly common. For some young people, though, offending is not simply part of 'normal' youthful activity but altogether more frequent and problematic. It is widely accepted that a comparatively small proportion of 'persistent' offenders account for a high proportion of all offences (see, for example, Farrington, 1996; Flood-Page *et al.*, 2000; Graham and Bowling, 1995; Hagell and Newburn, 1994). The question of identifying the minority of offenders who are most heavily involved in crime has become a key policy issue in Scotland, as elsewhere. Yet developing an appropriate method of identifying persistent offenders, and more particularly, the extent to which it is possible to predict who might become a persistent offender has been hotly debated, on methodological as well as moral and ethical grounds. Research conducted for the Home Office in the 1990s identified a series of problems in relation to identifying persistent offenders (Hagell and Newburn, 1994). First, different definitions of thresholds identify different individuals – there is no easily identifiable body of young people who are persistently offending. Second, much of the offending of those who admit to frequent offending, or who are more frequently arrested, is fairly transient in nature, and so by the time such young people have been identified, they may well have ceased their offending and been replaced by others. Third, attempts to predict who may become persistent tend to be highly inaccurate, and often result in the identification of 'false positives' (or those identified as likely to go on to have extended criminal careers, but don't) and 'false negatives' (or those who are not identified as likely to go on to become extensive offenders, but who do) (Hagell and Newburn, 1994).

Different jurisdictions have adopted different measurement criteria. As discussed in Chapter 4, the Scottish government announced measures designed to give a more rounded and reliable picture of young people's offending behaviour and provide an indicator of persistent young offenders. The Executive's 10 Point Action Plan on Youth Crime (2002c) defined a persistent young offender as someone with five or more referrals to the Children's Reporter on offence grounds in a six-month period. According to SCRA figures, the average number of offences per young person referred to the Children's Reporter has increased in recent years. The Scottish data show that the number of persistent young offenders increased nationally by 16% between 2003/4 and 2005/6 from 1201 to 1388. More recent data show a continuing rise in numbers with an increase nationally by a further 3% from 1388 to 1429 (SCRA, 2007).

In 2005/6, SCRA published research on the backgrounds and circumstances of persistent young offenders in Scotland (Bradshaw, 2005). The research identified that: problematic substance misuse was evident in over half (56%) of the cases studied; almost all of the children studied experienced problematic issues with their schooling or education (93% were failing to achieve in terms of educational attainment); almost three-quarters (73%) were reported to have experienced problems with parental or family relationships; and almost three-quarters (72%) of the sample had been initially referred to the Reporter on a non-offence (care and protection) related matter (Bradshaw, 2005, p. 3). Of course, while it is important to acknowledge the common characteristics and high levels of need within the young offender population, it is equally important to acknowledge the variations in the needs and characteristics of different individual offenders who may have different patterns of offending. For example, the research literature on females who offend shows that while male and female offenders share some universal needs and characteristics, there are also key differences between them (McIvor, 2004; Batchelor and Burman, 2004).

Young people and self-reported offending

Given the doubts about the validity and selectivity of official statistics, researchers have increasingly turned to other sources of information about offending behaviour. One such means is that provided by self-report studies in which people are asked directly about their involvement in offending and other forms of rule-breaking behaviour, whether this was detected or not. Such studies provide an estimate of offending unaffected by selection and processing by the criminal justice system (Graham and Bowling, 1995), and have the benefit of including criminal activity that has not resulted in detection and conviction. Self-report studies have been used not only to gain a 'truer' picture of offending, but also as a means of shedding light on why offending occurs, and the degree to which it correlates with other social factors, particularly gender, race and socio-economic position (Muncie, 1999). On the whole, such studies tend to focus on less serious law-breaking behaviour, such as acquisitive and expressive property offences (e.g. vandalism, theft), although some have investigated violent offences (e.g. threats, fights, use of weapon). They have been used mainly in relation to young people (e.g. Flood-Page *et al.*, 2000; Graham and Bowling, 1995; Jamieson *et al.*, 1999), and most conclude that youth offending is more widespread in the population than may be revealed by official statistics, while at the same time challenging commonly held conceptions about offender characteristics (Coleman and Moynihan, 1996, p. 67). Yet, and importantly, it is also evident from the many self-report studies that have been undertaken that most young people are not involved in crime. For those who do commit offences, the evidence from both reconviction and self-report studies has consistently indicated that the great majority 'grow out' of it (MORI, 2001).

A criticism often levelled at self-report studies is that of reliability in relation to self-reports of delinquency by young people, although there is now a considerable body of literature which indicates a consistently high level of truthfulness among respondents (see Hindelang *et al.*, 1981; Huizinga and Elliot, 1986; Junger-Tas, 1994).

Although, unlike other countries, Scotland does not maintain a nationally representative survey of self-report offending, there are several rich sources of Scottish self-report data (see Anderson *et al.*, 1994; Jamieson *et al.*, 1999; Smith and McVie, 2003). The Edinburgh Study of Youth Transitions and Crime, a major longitudinal study of a cohort of over 4,000 young people who commenced secondary school in Edinburgh in 1998, is a prominent exemplar. The young people participating in the study complete a self-report questionnaire that includes questions about their experience of offending and anti-social behaviour. Information has been collected over six annual sweeps from a range of sources, including questionnaires completed by cohort members, school records, and files held by police juvenile liaison officers, the Reporter and the social work department. At each sweep of the study, the period covered is the previous 12 months (with the exception of sweep 1, in which the reference period was 'ever'), so that the study provides a continuous account of events in the lives of the young people in the cohort. Key themes covered in the questionnaire are: self-reported offending and drug and alcohol use; experience of victimisation; friendship patterns, gang membership and friends' offending; leisure activities, including hanging around; family structure and parenting; school experience; contacts with the police and youth justice agencies; neighbourhood dynamics; and a number of personality variables such as self-esteem and impulsivity (Smith and McVie, 2003). While it is confined to Edinburgh, the study provides much useful information on the prevalence and incidence rates of various types of crimes and offences committed by young people, which is generally reflective of the broader Scottish population.

Evidence from self-report studies show gender differences persist, in that fewer females than males admit ever committing an offence, while at the same time indicate that the difference between young male and young female offending rates may be less than that suggested by official figures (e.g. Anderson *et al.*, 1994; Flood-Page *et al.*, 2000; Jamieson *et al.*, 1999). Jamieson *et al.* (1999) found that while girls were less likely than boys to report committing offences, and they reported doing so less frequently, they nonetheless found that 94% of boys and 82% of girls in their sample of young people admitted that they had committed one or more offences, with most claiming to have done so within the previous 12 months (85 % of boys and 67 % of girls) (Jamieson *et al.*,1999, p. 12). Although the types of offending were not very serious, there was a striking similarity in the offences reportedly committed by boys and girls, with 56% of girls and 69% of boys reported damaging property, 53% of girls as opposed to 66% of boys reported shoplifting, and 49% of girls reported being involved in a street fight, compared to 68% of boys.

The Edinburgh Study suggests that 'there is a substantial difference between boys and girls in levels of serious delinquency, but a relatively small difference in levels of broad delinquency, including trivial as well as serious incidents'. The gender gap in offending appears to be smallest at around 14 years but then begins to diverge again. Specific offences associated with girls are theft from their home, writing graffiti, and truancy; carrying a weapon, burglary, robbery, theft from cars and cruelty to animals were found to be much more common among boys. An important finding is that there are substantial differences between the explanatory models needed in relation to serious delinquency in boys and girls. It is suggested that 'broad delinquency tends to be limited to adolescence, whereas serious offending is more likely to persist throughout the life course, and to be caused by deep-seated neuropsychological deficits, which are more common in boys than girls' (Smith and McAra, 2004).

Victimisation Data

The Scottish Crime and Victimisation Survey (SCVS), previously known as the Scottish Crime Survey (SCS), is a household survey of people's experiences and perceptions of crime. The SCVS monitors the extent of victimisation by asking respondents (aged 16 and over) resident in private households about their experiences of most types of personal and household crime, and, to some extent, provides an alternative and complementary measure of crime to the police recorded crime statistics. It collects information about people's experiences of and attitudes towards a range of crime-related issues, such as the impact of crime on victims, public anxieties and reactions to crime, and attitudes towards the police and other parts of the criminal justice system.

Scottish crime survey data reflect some of the above general trends found in the official statistics of reported and recorded crime. Indeed victimisation data suggest that crime was falling during the early to mid-1990s, and, although there have been some fluctuations in the overall estimates since then, the most recent crime survey (2005/6) indicates that crime victimisation levels are back to around the levels recorded in 1992. Most of the increase between 2004 and 2005/6 is accounted for by a rise in minor assaults (Brown and Bolling, 2007). Furthermore, a growing proportion of people in Scotland perceive crime rates in their local area to be relatively stable (Brown and Bolling, 2007).

The data can be used to examine trends in the level and nature of crime over time and assess varying crime risks. However, victimisation surveys generally offer little information about the age of offenders, since victims often do not know who is responsible for the crimes they experience. There was a small add-on to the Scottish survey in 2000 of just over 400 young people aged between 12 and 15 years, which covered young people's offending behaviour, their worries about specific crimes and the likelihood to report victimisation. But meaningful analysis of this additional survey was hampered due to high levels of non-response to many of the questions, particularly those relating to offending behaviour.

It is important to remember that offenders and victims of crime are not always discrete categories. Nearly all children have been victims of crime at least once, according to a survey of more than 3,000 children between 1997 and 2006, carried out by the Howard League for Penal Reform (2007). While not specifically focused on Scotland, the poll found that 95% of young people had suffered some kind of victimisation, including nearly three-quarters (72 %) who had been assaulted. In 2003, the Glasgow Youth Survey was undertaken in response to issues raised by school pupils in Glasgow (MORI Scotland, 2003).It was aimed at gauging the opinions, feelings and experiences of young people aged 11–18 in mainstream education in terms of their current lifestyle and future plans. Just over 1,500 young people took part, through a self-completion questionnaire. A number of the topics covered related to crime and anti-social behaviour. While the sample is relatively small and in no way representative, nonetheless the findings offer useful insights into young people's fear of crime and concerns about personal safety, their experience of being a victim of crime and their experience in committing various types of crime. Seventeen per cent reported feeling very safe in areas around where they live and almost half felt fairly safe. However, a quarter reported that they did not feel very safe and one in ten 'not at all safe' in their local area. Three in five young respondents said they felt very or fairly worried about being attacked in the street or other public place. In terms of experiences of victimisation, over half (55%) stated that something negative had happened to them in the last year. Being threatened by others (39% of respondents) was the most commonly mentioned incident. One in five (18%) said they had been physically attacked in the past year. Boys were more likely than girls to have experienced some sort of incident: half (48%) said they had been threatened by others compared with around three in ten girls (29%). The likelihood of being a victim of crime also increases with age: more than half of boys aged between 14 and 18 claimed to have been threatened by others and a third said they had been physically attacked in the last year (MORI Scotland, 2003).

Conclusions

So what to make of this rather cloudy picture? The data sources are limited; any single data source used on its own cannot provide sufficient detail. The best official estimate currently available draws on several data sources, including recorded crime statistics and SCRA data and court data on criminal proceedings, as well as secondary data sources (DTZ Pieda, 2005). These estimates calculate that just over 40% of all crimes and offences in Scotland are attributable to young people under the age of 21, which means that almost 60% of crime and offences are attributable to those over 21 years. Youth crime rates have decreased steadily in recent years, in line with overall decreases. Most youth crime is theft-related. Young people are responsible for higher proportions of offences such as fire-raising, vandalism, theft of motor vehicles, theft by opening lock-fast places, handling offensive weapons and housebreaking. Young people seem less likely to commit crimes of indecency, other crimes of dishonesty such as fraud and reset and motor vehicle offences. Under-15-year-olds commit approximately a third of youth crime, with the remainder attributable to those aged 16–17 years. The vast majority of youth crime is committed by males.

The data do not suggest that youth crime in Scotland is rising in an uncontrollable way, as media hyperbole sometimes tends to suggest. Indeed, the evidence on young people and crime would seem to contradict the representation of popular perception by the media. Indeed, as noted by Furlong and Cartmel (1997), if one were to consider crime from a young person's point of view, what might be most worrying about crime statistics is that young people are much more likely to be victims than perpetrators of crime.

Note

1 It should be noted that the Scottish Government classification of non-sexual crimes of violence include homicide, serious assault, robbery and (pre-2001) handling offensive weapons. Crimes of indecency include sexual assault (from 2002 sub-categorised as rape and attempted rape, indecent assault), lewd and indecent behaviour. Crimes of dishonesty include housebreaking, theft by opening a lock-fast place, theft of a motor vehicle, shoplifting, other theft and fraud, and 'other' crimes include crimes against public justice, drugs, and (2001 onwards) handling offensive weapons.

CHAPTER 4

Youth Justice: Policy, Research and Evidence

Fergus McNeill

Introduction

This short chapter is in three parts. The first section provides a broadly chronological account of some of the key developments in Scottish youth justice policy since devolution. The second section contains an examination of the available research evidence about the impact of some of the main youth justice policy initiatives. The concluding section discusses the meaning and role of research evidence in youth justice in Scotland and asks to what extent Scotland's approach can be said to be 'evidence-based'.[1]

Youth justice: developments since devolution

There are two obvious reasons for this chapter's focus on the period since devolution. The first is pragmatic, in that space would not permit us to look back further and that it will be challenging enough to try to summarise what has been a period of frenetic – some might even say frenzied – activity in this field since 1999. The second reason is related and, with the benefit of hindsight, seems obvious. Devolution has fundamentally changed political debate about crime and justice in Scotland and youth justice has provided signal evidence of this change. Whereas prior to devolution the 'constitutional question' defined Scottish political parties (or Scottish branches of UK political parties) and differentiated those that stood on similar social democratic terrain, with the constitutional question effectively settled (at least between 1999 and 2007), these same parties had to find new ways to shape their electoral identities. As has become lamentably common in western democracies in the last three or four decades (see Garland, 2001), in Scotland this led to a new and rapid politicisation of crime and justice. Though it would take a much more detailed and critical analysis than can be provided here, it could be argued that Scotland has seen the emergence of what Jonathan Simon has recently referred to as 'governing through crime' (Simon, 2007).

The Youth Crime Review

The sea-change began in 1999 when the Government announced its commitment to review youth justice, and set up an Advisory Group on Youth Crime to assess the extent and effectiveness of options available to the Children's Hearings System and the criminal courts involving persistent young offenders. Their report identified responses to 14- to18-year-old offenders as requiring most attention (Scottish Executive, 2000a), and put forward recommendations for a strategic multi-agency approach which would seek to balance the needs of the 16- and 17-year-old offenders with public concern over the need to address offending behaviour, particularly for what was understood to be a relatively small number of persistent offenders (estimated to be about 2,300 young people) responsible for a significant amount of offending (estimated to be 25% of all crime). Although the Hearing System can deal with young people up to the age of 18 years, in practice most young offenders of 16 and 17 are dealt with in the adult criminal system. The short and much-travelled journey between the two systems involves a dramatic shift from the holistic 'needs-based' approach of the Hearings system to an institutionally and conceptually different system whose main goal is punishment (McNeill and Batchelor, 2002; 2004).

While the Report's recommendations were broadly accepted, they were never fully realised. The arrival in November 2001 of Jack McConnell as New Labour's third First Minister resulted in the development of a more punitive, correctionalist agenda, with a 'toughening-up' of policy towards young offenders. The tone was set early in McConnell's administration when the 'bridging pilot' proposed by the review group – a pilot to explore extending a more fully resourced Hearings system to cover 16- and 17-year-olds (thus diverting them from the adult system) – was unceremoniously dropped; proposals to raise the age of criminal responsibility from 8 to 12 were simply ignored.

The Audit Scotland Report

At the same time as a more punitive, correctionalist tone began to be evident in government discourses about youth crime a more managerialist strand of thinking also emerged, principally in a series of reports by Audit Scotland. In the first of these reports, *Youth Justice in Scotland: A Baseline Report* (2001), Audit Scotland, having reviewed some of the evidence about levels of youth crime in Scotland and its associated costs, outlined the ways in which they intended to measure progress in the youth justice system by examining:

- existing information on the time taken for under- and over-16s to go through different stages in the two systems, in order to identify good practice and opportunities to reduce unnecessary delay;
- the extent to which assessment methods used to identify the needs of individual offenders follow accepted good practice;
- following assessment, the extent to which identified needs are met through relevant programmes (for example, to address offending behaviour, or to meet educational, training or health needs);
- the extent to which the risks to society from offenders are assessed against existing good practice standards, and whether recommendations are acted upon;
- whether decision-makers have the information they require to make sound decisions regarding individuals, and whether managers have the necessary information to plan and manage their services effectively;
- the financial framework underpinning youth justice systems in Scotland, and the costs of different interventions.

In 2002, Audit Scotland's subsequent assessment of the operation of the youth justice system – *Dealing with Offending by Young People* (Audit Scotland, 2002) – provided sobering reading. They reported that it took 5.5 months on average for an offence referral to reach a Hearing (and 7.5–8.5 months for court decisions) and that there were significant variations in decision making in different areas. The proportion of offence grounds referred to Hearings by Reporters varied between 10% and 47%; Procurators Fiscals' rates of 'no further action' decisions on under-21s varied between 1% and 17%. The percentage of under-21s convicted and sentenced to detention varied from 3% to 24%. There were also wide variations in service provision – Audit Scotland (2002) estimated that 400 children were not getting services they needed. They also noted problems with a lack of specialist services for persistent offenders and a lack of qualified social work staff. Indeed, they reported major staffing problems in social work, noting a 13% vacancy rate among children's services social workers at that time (that is, a shortfall of 183 workers). They also suggested that social workers needed better training to work more effectively with young people who offend. In terms of the use of financial resources, they found that only 37% of the money spent on youth justice (£240 million) was spent on service delivery; 63% was spent on reaching decisions.

Scotland's Action Programme to Reduce Crime

At the same time as domestic scrutiny was producing such challenging findings, international observers from the UN Committee on the Rights of the Child in 2002 commented favourably on Scotland's approach to youth justice, apart from the low age (8 years) of criminal responsibility. However, the confluence of punitive discourses, concerned with the system's alleged 'softness' on offenders, and managerialist discourses, concerned with its alleged inefficiencies and ineffectiveness, produced a powerful driver for further change (see McAra, 2006). The Executive's response was *Scotland's Action Programme to Reduce Youth Crime* (Scottish Executive, 2002b). The Action Programme, in fact, was published shortly before the second Audit Scotland report, but it clearly anticipated many of that report's findings. The action programme very clearly reiterated the previous emphasis on addressing persistent offending by developing effective practice and it signalled the arrival of national standards for youth justice (more of which below). Taking forward a key recommendation of the Executive's earlier review of youth crime (Scottish Executive, 2000a), the action programme required that 'what works' principles should be incorporated into an expanded range of services and interventions for persistent offenders, and that all of these would be accessible to the Hearings System, and the criminal prosecution services alike (Scottish Executive, 2000a, para. 19).

The 'what works' paradigm has led to government prioritisation of 'evidence-based' policy and practice, investment in certain types of research and evaluation, and the promotion of accredited programmes for offenders (see McNeill, 2006). 'What works' offender programmes are focused on targeting offender behaviour by tackling criminogenic need (rather than generic welfare needs) and tend to involve planned intervention, over a specified period of time, characterised by a sequence of activities designed to achieve clearly defined objectives. Because 'what works' programmes are aimed at behavioural change, they may be seen as rehabilitative in nature, yet because they prioritise and target risk factors for offending behaviour, rather than the needs of the offender, they have the potential to undermine the more child-centred approach adopted by social work services. The focus in 'what works' programmes on addressing risk factors (and on matching the level and type of intervention to the level and type of risk) necessitates a concomitant emphasis on risk assessment. Social workers in Scotland are therefore now expected to undertake risk assessment using standardised assessment tools (ASSET/YLS-I) for all offence referrals proceeding to a Children's Hearing.

In addition to the emphasis on developing 'evidence-based practice', *Scotland's Action Programme to Reduce Youth Crime* included a 10 Point Action Plan on Youth Crime which set out a range of measures to tackle persistent offending (Scottish Executive, 2002c). These included the development of a pilot scheme of Fast Track Hearings for offenders under 16 years, a pilot Youth Court for persistent offenders aged 16 to 17 years and a review of the scope for imposing Anti-Social Behaviour Orders, Community Service Orders and Restriction of Liberty Orders on persistent young offenders, all of which have been subsequently introduced. The 10 Point Plan acknowledged the need to tackle, not just the crime itself, but its underlying causes. It had five aims:

- to increase public confidence in the youth justice system;
- to give victims a greater stake;
- to ease the transition between youth justice and adult court systems;
- to provide all young people with the opportunity to fulfil their potential;
- to promote early intervention with young children as a preventive measure.

The National Standards and the National Target

The action plan also prioritised the establishment of the National Standards for Scotland's Youth Justice Services (Scottish Executive, 2002a), which were duly published in 2002. The standards set out a series of objectives aimed at improving the quality of the youth justice process and services for children and young people in Scotland. The standards entail more than procedural compliance; by also implying objectives they have clear implications for the nature of the services required and for the ways in which effectiveness should be assessed. Critically, the standards set a specific target for youth justice services in Scotland: to reduce the numbers of persistent offenders by 10% by 2006 and by a further 10% by 2008. The persistence criteria required five episodes of offending in a six-month period. The reasons given for targeting young people who offend persistently were not only that they account for a disproportionate quantity of offences, but they were also growing in number by contrast with a stable pattern for infrequent offenders (SCRA, 2006). Furthermore, Children's Hearings Panel members and professionals involved in the Hearings system believed it worked least well for young people who offend seriously or persistently (Hallett *et al.*, 1998), and that there was a risk of such offenders graduating to adult court (Waterhouse *et al.*, 2000). A baseline data report indicated the extent of the challenge faced by all those involved in reducing persistent offending by young people, and simultaneously provided the basis for performance management information (PA Consulting, 2004). The baseline report showed that 7% of young people referred to the Reporter on offence grounds were persistent offenders as defined, and that group was responsible for a third of offence referrals (2004, pp. 3–4). The relatively small number of young people involved in persistent offending (between 1,300 and 1,400) are seen to be responsible for a disproportionate level of crime and anti-social behaviour in a number of local communities throughout Scotland (SCRA, 2006, p. 9).

Though concerns about persistent offenders were and remain legitimate, arguably the national target was misconceived from the outset; whereas the policy emphasis was on making the system more effective in delivering reduced re-offending as an *outcome*, the target in fact captured *inputs* to the system. From the outset, the flow of young people into the system was likely to be vulnerable to a combination of increased public concern, media hype, new resources and governmental pressure on services to intervene more swiftly, more often and (they hoped) more effectively. Leaving aside any changes in the level of youth offending (and there is little evidence that it has risen in Scotland in recent years), these factors were always likely to increase levels of *formal* action in the system – and a more active system was always likely to increase the risk of more young people triggering the persistence criteria. As stated in Chapter 3, it is also likely that changes to the Scottish Crime Reporting Standard in 2004, which required the police to formally record more minor crimes, also helped to increase the numbers of detected crimes involving young people. Predictably, therefore, rather than declining, the number of persistent offenders rose from 1,201 to 1,429 (an increase of 19%) between 2003/4 and 2006/7 (Audit Scotland, 2007).

Leaving the target aside, the significant toughening of the policy (and, through the standards, the increased regulation around its implementation) was broadly seen as evidence both that McConnell regarded youth crime as a key issue for the election and that he considered the existing line to be too 'soft'. Scottish Labour duly took an aggressive approach to tackling what came to be described as 'ned crime' in the Scottish Parliamentary election campaign of 2003. Youth crime and disorder were among the most prominent issues of the campaign with Labour proposals for Parenting Orders underwritten by the threat of imprisonment for parents who failed to control their children being among the most controversial of their manifesto pledges. Though optimistic critics hoped that this proposal represented opportunistic electioneering and was designed to be 'sacrificed' in coalition talks, it survived in the partnership agreement between Labour and the Liberal Democrats (Scottish Executive, 2003a) alongside plans to introduce Anti-Social Behaviour Orders for the under-16s and promises to provide 'sufficient' secure accommodation and electronic monitoring of young offenders. These measures were subsequently introduced in the Anti-Social Behaviour (Scotland) Act 2004, which is addressed in some detail in a separate chapter of this volume.

The Youth Justice Improvement Programme

Though the focus following the 2003 election shifted subtly (and problematically) from youth justice to anti-social behaviour, a further attempt to stimulate change arrived in November 2005, with the establishment of the multi-agency Youth Justice Improvement Group. In October 2006, the group produced a Youth Justice Improvement Programme which ran until March 2008. The programme identified five success criteria for a youth justice system: to reduce offending and anti-social behaviour by young people; to stop young people getting to the stage where their behaviour causes serious problems; to take strong action to stop such behaviour and reduce its impact on others; to tackle the causes of such behaviour and turn round the lives of these young people; and to reassure communities that effective action is being taken to address behaviour and offending issues (Scottish Executive, 2006h). It also identified the mechanisms through which these criteria might be met:

- supporting parents;
- making sure that young people have positive things to do and opportunities;
- spotting early warning signs, from the youngest age, and tackling the root causes;
- taking action to prevent a repetition of that behaviour and protect others from it;
- taking action to tackle the causes of that behaviour;

- taking action for as long as the behaviour (or the risk) persists;
- cooperation between agencies;
- using interventions and programmes that are known to be effective;
- ensuring that barriers to change (poor mental health, addictions, poor education) are tackled;
- effective communication about action and outcomes (Scottish Executive, 2006h).

Audit Scotland (2007) pithily observed that all 'five areas in the improvement programme echo recommendations we made in 2002 and 2003... and earlier commitments made by the Executive (i.e., those included in the ten-point action plan and national standards), reflecting the limited progress the Executive has achieved in securing effective implementation of policy in this area' (p. 8). More generally, if Audit Scotland's 2002 report was sobering, its 2007 report made for depressing reading. The headline conclusion of the report was that although youth justice funding had increased from £235 million in 2000/1 to over £330 million in 2005/6, the impact of the additional funding (and of the plethora of initiatives described only in part above) on improving services and outcomes had not been demonstrated and only limited progress had been made in the five years between the two reports. On the positive side, Audit Scotland (2007) recognised that the national standards had provided a focus for improved working across and between agencies; that the police and the Reporters had improved the speed of their decision making; that more services were available and that 500 new children's service social workers were in place. However, they also noted gaps in performance data, new tensions created by the introduction of ASBOs as an alternative means of addressing young people's behaviour, pressures on the Hearings System brought about by increased referrals, variation in police referral practice, lack of progress in the speed of provision of social work reports, and lack of evidence about sustained reductions in youth offending. As the press were keen to report, this seemed like a limited return on an investment of £100 million.

Youth justice and the Nationalists

In 2007, the Scottish National Party achieved a narrow victory in the Scottish Parliamentary election. Unlike their predecessor administrations which, by dint of Labour/Liberal Democrat coalitions, secured clear majorities in the

Parliament, the SNP's is a minority administration, meaning that they have to govern by consensus. Equally importantly, as a nationalist party which aims to imbue the Scottish people with the self-confidence required to vote for independence in a planned referendum, unlike their predecessors they have a clear electoral interest in 'talking up' Scotland's young people. Although the current Cabinet Secretary for Justice, Kenny MacAskill, seems to recognise the political risks of being seen to be soft on crime, his public statements on youth crime and justice differ clearly from those of his predecessors. Thus far at least, the targets of his rhetoric have not been young people but rather the culture of 'booze and blades' or the three Ds of 'drink, drugs and deprivation'. Though it is perhaps too early to surmise the SNP Government's longer-term agenda on youth crime, the shift in direction is clear enough. The national target for reducing the number of persistent offenders has already been dropped and the Youth Justice Improvement Programme has been replaced by *Preventing Offending by Young People: A Framework for Action*, published in June 2008. Significantly, the new framework is a joint publication of Scottish Government, the Convention of Scottish Local Authorities, the Scottish Children's Reporters Administration, the Association of Chief Police Officers in Scotland and the Crown Office and Procurator Fiscal Service. Though the content of the framework document is familiar (in setting out a range of activities to address prevention, early and effective intervention, managing high risk, victims and community confidence and planning and performance improvement), there are subtle differences not just in the cooperation involved in its production but also in its tone. In the latter regard, the foreword (from the Minister for Community Safety *and* the COSLA spokesperson of children, young people and families) signals the shift in discourse:

> The vast majority of young people in Scotland make a positive contribution to society and are valuable and valued members of their communities. We want to build on the great qualities that young people bring to our society: energy, enthusiasm, creativity, an appetite for learning and huge potential for the future. At the same time, we must remove the barriers that prevent too many of our young people from realising their potential and leading successful, fulfilling lives… This Framework belongs to all the key partners who together are committed to preventing offending by young people. We share a vision of a Scotland where all children

and young people pursue their dreams and fulfil their potential in safe, strong and supportive families and communities... Together, we reject the polarisation of children's needs and community safety; we will champion both... The vision is a familiar one. What is new is our shared commitment... As equal partners, we will focus on identifying and embedding what works, enabling good practice to spread, and demonstrating impact in improved outcomes for children, young people and communities. At every level, we will get better at partnership, using information, seeing holistically and acting strategically. (Scottish Government, 2008g, p. 2)

It is notable that the term anti-social behaviour appears only once in the entire document, and that reference is in the context of a claim that success in youth justice cannot be measured by the numbers of persistent offenders or ASBOs.

Before going on to examine in more detail some of the evidence about what some of the previous Executive's initiatives did and did not achieve, it is important to note (since space prohibits the provision of any detail) that these developments in relation to youth justice need to be understood in the context of wider developments in relation to the Children's Hearing System and children's services in Scotland in recent years. Accounts of some of these developments are included elsewhere in this book.

Recent research on Scottish youth justice

In 2005/6, the Scottish Children's Reporters Administration published research on the backgrounds and circumstances of persistent young offenders in Scotland (Bradshaw, 2005). The research identified that: problematic substance misuse was evident in over half (56%) of the cases studied; almost all of the children studied experienced problematic issues with their schooling or education (93% were failing to achieve in terms of educational attainment); almost three-quarters (73%) were reported to have experienced problems with parental or family relationships; and almost three-quarters (72%) of the sample had been initially referred to the Reporter on a non-offence (care and protection) related matter (Bradshaw, 2005, p. 3). Such data are consistent with earlier studies of the needs, deeds and characteristics of persistent offenders in Scotland (McNeill and Batchelor, 2002) and in England and Wales (Liddle and Solanki, 2002). Though much more could be said about the complex and intense needs experienced by young people involved in persistent offending, the key point to note here is that, in the context of these intense and complex needs, enabling and supporting young people to change is likely to be far from simple.

Fast Track Hearings

It was partly to address this challenge that a Fast Track Hearings pilot was introduced in a number of sites in early 2003, specifically targeting persistent offenders under 16. Fast Track Hearings were distinguished from any other type of Children's Hearing by the speed with which referrals were processed. The main aim was to improve practice, processes and outcomes with respect to the ways that the Hearings System and associated services dealt with young people who persistently offend (as noted earlier, the persistence criteria involved five or more episodes of offending in a 6-month period). Particular objectives were: to speed up the time taken at each stage of decision making (and hence for young people to see the connection between their actions and the official response); promote more comprehensive assessments including appraisals of offending risk; ensure that all young people who persistently offend and who require an appropriate programme had access to one; and reduce re-offending rates as an overall result of the efforts made in such cases. An evaluation of the pilot showed that, in most respects, Fast Track was largely meeting its objectives, in that the findings were positive with regard to reduced time-scales and other aspects such as assessment and action plans (Hill *et al.*, 2005, p. 25). However, the evidence about the impact of the initiative on offending was mixed. For the 228 Fast Track referrals processed during the first 12 months of the pilot, the number of offences committed in the first 6 months following referral dropped by over 500 (23%). However, data from comparison sites where the specific procedures and resources associated with the Fast Track pilot did not apply revealed even better apparent performance. Thus, whereas for young people in the Fast Track sites the mean number of offences committed fell from 9.1 to 7.5 (n=167), in the comparator sites the mean number of offences dropped from 10.7 to 5 (n=56). Put another way, the percentage of young people who reduced their offending ranged from 50% to 82% in the pilot sites, but from 70% to 91% in the comparison sites.

In discussing these apparently perplexing findings, Hill *et al.* (2007a) are quick to note the limitations of the data, in particular rueing the fact that the Executive did not fund a self-report study of re-offending. They also note that the level of activity changed significantly in the pilot and comparison sites during the study: thus, although pilot and comparison sites had similar levels of offence referrals prior to the initiative (with the comparison sites processing 84% of the number of referrals processed in the pilot sites), offence referrals subsequently rose in the pilot sites by 42%, but by only 8% in the comparison sites. As a result, despite the additional resources provided for the initiative, *less* money was spent per case in the Fast Track sites than in the comparison sites. Hill *et al.* (2007a, p. 134) speculate that the success of the comparison areas might be explained partly by 'an emphasis on early intervention, the cumulative benefits of falling numbers of "difficult" cases allowing more to be spent per case and perhaps a better balance of direct work as opposed to assessment and report writing' (the latter being prioritised in Fast Track procedures).

Despite their own hesitancy about the real import of their study, Hill *et al.* (2007a) also note that:

> the Scottish Executive regarded the data on offending, despite its limitations, as conclusive. This suggested that the additional resources had not produced the desired reductions compared with elsewhere in Scotland, so 'Fast Track' was not rolled out nationally as had been intended. Instead the Executive decided to concentrate on seeking improvements in decision making and services by means of imposing National Standards. Interestingly, at about the same time, the review of the Children's Hearings that had been prompted by critical comments produced a largely positive report committed to the centrality of the child's welfare, while also recognizing the need for changes. (Hill *et al.*, 2007a, p. 135)

Youth Courts

It is interesting and instructive, perhaps even salutary, to compare the response to the largely positive, but inconclusive, Fast Track evaluation with the response to the evaluation of the pilot Youth Courts.

Despite overall falling youth crime rates, and despite the opportunity of sending 16- and 17-year-olds through the Children's Hearing System, the Scottish Executive opted to pilot a court-based approach and (re)introduced a designated Youth Court for 16- and 17-year-old persistent offenders in June 2003. This initiative was proposed as a means of 'easing the transition between the youth justice and adult justice system', and for increasing public confidence in Scotland's system of youth justice. It was initially established as a two-year pilot in one Sheriff Court, and following the evaluation of the pilot

(McIvor *et al.*, 2004), a second pilot Youth Court was incepted, even though the number of referrals to the Youth Court were far less than anticipated. The feasibility study estimated that around 600 cases would be referred in a year, whereas there were only 147 referrals involving 120 young people in the first six months of the pilot (McIvor *et al.*, 2006).

This development met with much criticism, not least because the processing in adult court of persistent 16- and 17-year-old offenders represents a stark deviation from a 'child-centred' and needs-oriented state apparatus for dealing with young offenders to one based on deeds and individual responsibility (Piacentini and Walters, 2006).

The objectives of the Youth Court were:

- to reduce the frequency and seriousness of re-offending by 16- and 17-year-old offenders, particularly persistent offenders (and some 15-year-olds are referred to the court);
- to promote the social inclusion, citizenship and personal responsibility of these young offenders while maximizing their potential;
- to establish fast track procedures for those young persons appearing before the Youth Court;
- to enhance community safety, by reducing the harm caused to individual victims of crime and providing respite to those communities that experience high levels of crime;
- to test the viability and usefulness of a Youth Court using existing legislation and to demonstrate whether legislative and practical improvements might be appropriate (Youth Court Feasibility Project Group, 2002).

The Youth Court possesses the same powers of sentencing as the adult summary court and, therefore, adjudicates with all the legal equivalence of an adult jurisdiction. There are two criteria for allocation to the Youth Court. One is 'persistent offending' and the definition used is 'at least three separate incidents of alleged offending in the previous six months' (including the current charge), which is somewhat different from and lesser than that used in the Fast Track Hearings. The other criteria for allocation are 'contextual criteria', used as an indication of risk, and which lead the police and/or the Procurator Fiscal to believe that the offender is vulnerable to progress to more serious offending that would diminish community safety. As pointed out by Piacentini and Walters (2006, p. 49) 'contextual criteria' emerges as a 'catch-all' category for referring young offenders who fail to meet notions of 'persistent offender' and the lack of clear definition gives rise to a lack of consensus between different professional groups as to how the referral criteria should be interpreted. The evaluations by McIvor *et al.* (2004; 2006) showed that, in reality, almost twice as many offenders were referred to the Youth Court on 'contextual' grounds than on the grounds that they were persistent offenders.

An important aspect of the Youth Court was the 'fast tracking' of cases. Targets were set to try to ensure that cases are processed more quickly than would happen in the normal working of the Sheriff Court. In the majority of cases, alleged offenders made their first appearance in court within 10 days of the date that the crime was committed. There was a rolling-up of pre-existing charges in order that offenders can be treated simultaneously for all alleged crimes committed in the same period. Designated sheriffs share the work in the Youth Court. Young offenders under the previous system perhaps saw a Sheriff for a few minutes before sentence was passed, after which the court no longer had any dealings with them. In the Youth Court, the dedicated Sheriff continues to have oversight of the offender's performance, allowing for sentences to be amended as necessary. There is a wide range of services and 'dedicated programmes' for offenders available in the Youth Court, including offending reduction programmes, addictions services, alcohol and drug awareness, family group conferences, and restorative justice services. These services are provided by a range of service providers through local authority social work departments.

Piacentini and Walters (2006), who were members of the team that conducted the evaluation, in a highly critical article that draws primarily on the views of sentencers and young people, reach the conclusion that the Youth Court embodies 'double bind' justice (taken from Muncie, 2004, p. 214) where young people in need of support become subject to fast-track punishment, supervision and increased regulation. They argue that the range of interventions and programmes at the disposal of the Youth Court are testimony to how the parameters of correction become entwined with inclusion norms that are delivered by authorities of expertise (2006, p. 49). They raise a series of concerns about 'violations of children's rights, due process, increased use of detention and net widening… [and] a seriously flawed process premised on actuarial justice' (2006, p. 55).

Nonetheless, they also recognise that some might support the development of the Youth Court as a mode of diversion because, in its absence, 16- and 17-year-olds would be processed in adult Sheriff Summary courts. However, Piacentini and Walters (2006, pp. 54–5) argue that:

16 and 17 year old offenders under the supervision of the Children's Hearing would almost always have had their case remitted back to the Hearing unless they had committed serious indictable offences. Indeed at Hamilton, there were a slightly higher proportion of cases at the youth court, in comparison to the Sheriff Summary Court, being admonished or remitted back to the Children's Hearing System (Popham *et al.*, 2005a). But at the same time, in comparison to the Sheriff Summary Court, the youth court made 'greater use of detention and community-based disposals and much less use of fines' (Popham *et al.*, 2005a, p. 46). This contradiction raises a key concern about the youth court's role in up-tariffing. Second, the youth court is simply an adult court setting masquerading as a fast-track youth process. In that sense, diversion is not achieved and Scotland remains one of the few countries in Europe that prosecutes its children in adult 'contexts'.

Though the Youth Courts make extensive use of the community sanctions and, no doubt, intend these sanctions to fit the circumstances of the case, if these sanctions do indeed represent 'up-tariffing', this raises possible concerns about consistency, proportionality in sentencing and increased risks of default. Leaving aside the normative arguments for keeping 16- and 17-year-olds out of adult courts (whether convened and described as youth courts or not), the key empirical question therefore, is whether the Youth Courts did indeed up-tariff offenders relative to the adult courts. Unfortunately, this is not a question that the evaluation could answer directly. Precisely because the Youth Courts deal with higher-tariff *persistent* offenders, one would expect the patterns of disposals imposed to differ from those imposed on *all* young offenders in adult courts. Moreover, one would expect the patterns of disposal to differ in precisely the manner that they do – higher-tariff offenders would be expected to attract more sentences involving supervision and greater use of custody. Popham *et al.* (2005) note that, in the Hamilton Sheriff Court, comparing the overall sentencing patterns in relation to 16- and 17-year-olds dealt with on summary procedures in 2002 (prior to the Youth Court) and in 2004 reveals no significant differences in sentencing patterns. So, although the Hamilton Youth Court may be more interventionist (perhaps even more correctionalist) than the adult courts, this may be an artefact of differences in the nature of its business caused by the referral criteria.

Though concerns about net-widening, up-tariffing, rights and due process may preoccupy critical criminologists, the lesson of the Fast Track Hearings evaluation was that the Executive was principally concerned with reconviction data. In this regard, the Hamilton Youth Court fared comparatively well; despite the fact that the target group was persistent offenders and that fast-tracking would increase the likelihood of their speedy reconviction, rates of reconviction within 6 months for young offenders appearing at Hamilton Youth Court were (at 16%) lower than those at comparison adult summary courts (at 21–26%). In the Executive's rush to laud the success of their flagship initiative, the research team's caution about the limitations of this data (in terms of short follow-up and relatively low numbers) (Piacentini and Walters, 2006) was ignored – just as in the case of the negative findings from the Fast Track evaluation.

Conclusion: evidence, policy and practice

The rejection of caution in the interpretation of the findings from both evaluations reviewed above might seem like a mere footnote in the story of developments in Scottish youth justice. However, it might alternatively be read as being symptomatic of the troubled relationship between evidence, policy and practice in this area. As other chapters in this book have shown, the development of a new agenda in youth justice in Scotland is not the product of any robust evidence about rising rates of youth crime or compelling evidence about the limitations of existing systems and approaches. Indeed, there is strong evidence that youth crime has been falling in recent decades (see, for example, Soothill *et al.*, 2008) and that the Children's Hearing system was not so much flawed in its design as in its resourcing and execution (see Whyte, 2007).

An impartial observer would surely conclude that the genesis of youth justice policy does not reside primarily in research evidence – nor does it take its form and direction principally from evidence. Though many of the policy statements and programmes reviewed above challenge *practitioners* to be evidence-based in their interventions, the same standards are not always applied to *policy* itself, except perhaps in the sense that policy is driven by evidence of popular appeal and electoral success. Sometimes it seems as if it is less what works in relation to tackling youth crime and delivering justice for young people than what works in responding to public concern and media hype. The irony here, as is perhaps revealed in the fates of the national target for youth justice and more generally in the fate of the former Executive in the 2007 election, is that there is more to government than meeting public anxiety with populist responses. Such responses are always likely to be ill-fated because, in pursuing political advantage by responding to public anxieties, and 'talking up' youth crime as a problem that government can solve through tougher measures, politicians miss the key points that every criminology 101 student comes to understand: systems of justice are poor mechanisms for controlling crime rates whose main drivers lie elsewhere (principally in problems of inequality), and increasing justice system activity is more likely to increase formally processed crime (and formally labelled offenders) than to decrease it. This is a point that the current Scottish Government does seem to have grasped to some extent, at least in so far as the tone and discourse around youth justice and young people appears to have changed since 2007. Again, there may be political as well as principled reasons for this: a nationalist government cannot really afford to be overly negative in its portrayal of the conduct, prospects and potential of the nation's young people – to do so would be to further damage the public confidence on which support for independence may ultimately depend.

If youth justice has been a context within which the construction (or at least the interpretation) of evidence has tended to follow rather than lead policy, then perhaps the fundamental challenge is to work out how to develop genuinely evidence-based and principled *policy* (as well as practice) in the highly charged political context that has followed devolution.

Note

1 For more comprehensive accounts of these developments, readers are referred to recent chapters by Burman *et al.* (2007) and Whyte (2007). This chapter draws heavily on Burman *et al.* (2007) and I am grateful to Michele Burman for permission to re-use some of the material here. Those interested in analyses of the meaning and significance of developments in Scottish youth justice would do well to read McAra (2004) and McAra (2006).

CHAPTER 5

Youth Justice: Outcomes

Jenny Johnstone

Introduction

This chapter considers the formal disposals available within the youth justice process in Scotland. There has been a shift towards introducing more community and diversionary strategies based on the view that prison is unable to deal adequately with offenders and people held for short periods of time. In 2006/7 nearly 7,000 offenders who received a custodial sentence had already accumulated between them 47,500 prior spells in prison and, as the Scottish Prisons Commission Report (2008) highlights, nearly one in six of these offenders had already been to prison on more than ten previous occasions. The Report found that prison was 'not about making ... people better or more sorry for what they have done' and that the cost of imprisoning offenders diverted resources 'from other areas essential to the health of society' (para. 6.2). The authors of the report suggest that community investment – in nurseries, schools, youth services and hospitals, for example – would in the longer term stand a better chance of reducing crime than prisons do by targeting the socio-economic factors that have been identified as instrumental in young people's involvement in criminal activity.

In many European jurisdictions penalties for crimes are determined by statute but this is not the case in Scotland. The combination of the Procurator Fiscal's discretion in terms of where the prosecution takes place, the powers and procedures of the particular court (i.e. High, Sheriff Solemn or Sheriff Summary and District), the sentencing framework of the court and the maximum penalties set down by Parliament provide guidance, but sentencers in Scotland have wide discretion to decide the appropriate sentence in each case.

The Children's Hearing System deals with children under the age of 16, and above that age young people are dealt with in the adult criminal justice process or Youth Court (in those areas where a Youth Court exists).

Detention

Where children aged over 8 and under 16 years have committed a very serious offence (such as murder), they will be referred to the Procurator Fiscal and prosecuted before a criminal court. This could culminate in one or more of a range of court-imposed sanctions. For those aged under 21 years, detention is the ultimate sanction available to the Scottish criminal courts (for those aged over 21 years, it is imprisonment). Young people aged between 16 and 21 years generally serve custodial sentences in Young Offender Institutions (YOIs), of which there are currently five in Scotland. Scotland has proportionately larger numbers of young people in custody than in European countries of a comparable size. However the recent Prisons Commission Report has made various recommendations recognising their age and stage of development and the possibility that young offenders may be negatively influenced by older prisoners. The Commission recommends that the Government explore options for detaining 16- and 17-year-olds in secure youth facilities separate from older offenders and from those under the age of 16. To bring Scotland into line with international conventions and to deal more appropriately and effectively with younger offenders, the Commission recommends that the Government re-examine the case for diverting 16- and 17-year-olds to Specialist Youth Hearings with a wider range of options than are presently available in the Children's Hearings System.

Custody and residential care

At the time of writing Scotland currently has provision of 94 secure places spread across the dedicated secure units, with about 90 young people in placement at any one time. Figures suggest that approximately 200–250 young people are placed in secure accommodation each year with two-thirds of those being placed there on the authority of a Children's Hearing. The remaining third are subject to a criminal court order, either serving a sentence for a serious crime or on remand. The majority are boys but girls typically account for more than a quarter, most being placed for welfare reasons rather than offending. The most recent statistics show that there was an average of 81 residents in secure accommodation throughout 2005/6 (87 in 2004/5 and 92 in 2003/4) and that half of all young people admitted to secure accommodation during the year were 15 years of age. Though there has been a decline in the use of secure accommodation for most age-categories, it has been increasingly employed for individuals aged 16 or over. Importantly, too, though long-term stays in secure accommodation are becoming rarer, very short-term stays (less than 1 month) are becoming more common.

In the case of *S* v. *Miller* (2001), judges in the Court of Session ruled that while the placing of a child in secure accommodation under the supervision of a local authority does amount to deprivation of the child's liberty in terms of Article 5 of the UN Convention on the Rights of the Child, this is justified for the purposes of 'educational supervision' of a minor in terms of Article 5(1) (d). This arose from recognition by the Court of two significant points. First, the requirement of the Children's Hearing to hold the child's welfare as their paramount consideration in making any decision and, second, the obligation on managers of secure establishments in Regulation 4 of the Secure Accommodation (Scotland) Regulations 1996 to 'ensure that the welfare of a child placed and kept in such accommodation is safeguarded and promoted and that the child receives such provision in his education, development and control as is conducive to his best interests'. In 2006, the Scottish Executive published a report looking at increasing an understanding of the use and effectiveness of secure accommodation in relation to young people placed on the authority of a Children's Hearing. The decision in favour of secure accommodation is made on the grounds that the current level of risk that the young person poses cannot be safely managed within the community or an open setting. Some of the factors in making that decision include knowledge of what meets the best interests of that particular young person but also more fundamentally the availability of resources and expertise within local areas to manage young people and fully meet their individual needs. Differential experiences through a variety of methods employed by institutions were also a key finding:

> factors including the distance from the young people's home area, whether the unit catered primarily for young people who offend or who are at risk and whether the predominant underpinning ethos was to support emotional development through providing nurturing care or increase cognitive understanding and so help young people control their behaviour. (Scottish Executive, 2006c, p. 7)

A critical, and pertinent, finding was ensuring that individual needs are met – if they are not then placements could be ineffective and detrimental. The

Insight 33 Report on Secure Accommodation in Scotland (SEED, 2006) concluded that in the 'short term, secure accommodation had certainly kept some young people safe, and for most there were clear educational and health benefits' (2006, p. 11) but they found 'merit' in considering more open and community-based alternatives rather than pursuing secure accommodation, which gives rise to labelling and stigmatising the young person. The Report also found that the alternative sample included young persons who were 'managing and coping' without any secure accommodation provisions despite having 'longstanding' issues and difficulties (2006, p. 11). Open and community-based alternatives, therefore, also merit further development. Intensive community-based support, specialist fostering and close support residential provision are a few of the community-based disposals that have been developed before and after the Report was published. For example, the Intensive Support and Monitoring (Scotland) Regulations 2005 came into force in April 2005 and have been subsequently evaluated (referred to later in this chapter). What is imperative is that there is a recognised 'joined-up' or multi-agency and partnership approach to ensuring that these programmes meet 'directly' the needs of the young people involved.

Children on unruly certificates

The Criminal Procedure (Scotland) Act 1995 s51(1)(bb) provides for the detention of a child under 16 years of age but above 14 years of age, facing a criminal charge before the court, to be committed to a remand centre, prison or Young Offender Institution where the court deems the child to be 'unruly or depraved'. The Statistical Bulletin (Scottish Executive, 2007) provides details of the number of unruly certificates received in 2006/7. The number had increased to 33 from 28 in 2005/6. The majority (91%) were given to males with the age tending to be 15. Crimes of violence were the most common crimes for which they were used although there was variety. The average time spent in custody (before sentence, if any) was 16 days in 2006/7, a decrease from 17 days in 2005/6. During 2006/7, 70% of those receiving an unruly certificate spent less than 14 days in custody. In 2008 HM Chief Inspector of Prisons, Dr Andrew McLellan, raised concerns about the use of unruly certificates, suggesting that it was out of line with the UN Convention of the Rights of the Child. For children under the age of 16 who require restrictions on their movement because of potential danger to themselves or others it was proposed that a care environment should be provided that meets the needs of the individual, preferring that prison should be used for those who need to be there (Scottish Government, 2008g). The recent Criminal Justice and Licensing Bill (2009) proposes the removal of unruly certificates whereby young people are detained in adult prisons alongside adult prisoners. This is primarily an attempt to ensure that children do not suffer the adverse effects of being remanded in adult prisons. Local authorities may recognise that a welfare-oriented approach is more likely to have a positive impact on the behaviour of the offender; however, they may also be mindful of the fact that providing secure accommodation has huge cost and resource implications, and would rather fund or rely on voluntary organisations to support community-based initiatives.

Structured deferred sentences

The pilot Youth Courts have made extensive use of 'structured deferred sentences' (SDSs), commonly used in the adult criminal court. The SDS enables the young person to engage with the social work department for a period before returning to court for final sentencing. Regular programmes can be included to demonstrate that s/he has changed their behaviour. After the successful completion of the programme(s), the offender returns to court and the expectation is that s/he will be admonished. The value of this sentence to the court is that it allows some work to be done to address offending behaviour without attaching a criminal conviction to the offender. The danger, of course, is that the offender is receiving a punishment which is disproportionate to the seriousness of the offence and that failure to complete the programmes to the satisfaction of the court may lead to an additional sentence. The evaluation of structured deferred sentences concluded that most criminal justice professionals were positive about the use of deferred sentences, with a view that they were mainly seen as an alternative to probation (Macdivitt, 2008, p. 39). Similarly in the evaluation of the Airdrie Youth Court Pilot, thirteen referrals resulted in a structured deferred sentence being imposed. The mean age of the young offenders referred was 16.4 years at first referral. Two of these young people were subject to supervision requirements at the time they were referred to the Youth Court. The Report identified that social workers would have welcomed greater use of structured deferred sentences in some cases to enable a shorter, more focused period of intervention than would be possible with probation.

Imposition of ASBOs

Very few ASBOs have been imposed on young people in Scotland, although almost three-quarters of Antisocial Behaviour Contracts (ABCs) currently involve young people under 16. In late 2006, the Scottish Executive published the results of a survey of Local Authorities and Housing Associations that focused on the use of ASBOs in 2005/6 (DTZ and Heriot Watt University, 2007). In that year, 344 ASBO applications in total were submitted to the courts. Well over half of all ASBO subjects were aged over 26 years, while just over a tenth were aged 18 or under. Four ASBOs were granted in respect of 12–15 year olds, as Table 5.1 shows.

Table 5.1: Persons subject to ASBOs granted in 2005/6: breakdown by age and gender

Age Group	Female (%)	Male (%)	All (%)
12–15 years	0	2	1
16–18 years	6	16	12
19 –25 years	31	28	29
26 years and over	63	54	57
Total	100	100	100

Note: figures may not sum to 100% due to rounding.
Source: DTZ survey (2006).

As well as recording the number of ASBOs granted in relation to young people, the survey also collated cases involving young people where the Local Authority had 'actively considered' an ASBO application to the court. In all, 98 cases were reported to have been considered during 2005/6 and, of these, six were considered and approved as applications to the court, 61 were considered and subsequently rejected, while 31 remained unresolved at the time of the survey. Survey respondents were asked about the reasons for decisions not to proceed with court applications in cases involving young people. Overwhelmingly, the main reason was that, following examination, alternative measures were considered to be more appropriate. This suggests that agencies are taking time to consider all possible options for young people involved in anti-social behaviour, seeking ASBOs only when other options are seen to have failed. Decisions not to proceed solely due to lack of support from the Children's Hearing System or insufficient evidence were reported to be extremely rare. Local authorities reported making extensive use of alternative measures to counter anti-social behaviour involving young people. Cited examples included Anti-Social Behaviour Contracts (ABCs), parental agreement contracts, intensive support, parenting classes, mediation, diversionary activities, referrals to other agencies such as the Children's Hearing System or social services, community wardens and police notices. The range

Table 5.2 Persons (excluding companies) with a charge proved by main result, age and sex 1996–2006.

	1996/97	1997/98	1998/99	1999/00	2000/01	2001/02	2002/03	2003/04	2004/05	2005/06
TOTAL 1	150,783	148,614	136,506	127,526	112,832	121,248	127,410	133,124	134,493	128,091
Custody 2	16,937	16,299	16,027	15,894	15,656	16,494	17,320	16,567	16,697	15,967
Males Total 3	16,094	15,434	15,059	14,884	14,723	15,368	16,103	15,266	15,323	14,711
Under 21	4,765	4,371	4,327	4,056	3,979	3,773	3,518	3,184	2,997	3,105
21-30	7,324	6,955	6,664	6,985	6,850	7,338	7,889	7,483	7,241	6,428
Over 30	4,004	4,108	4,066	3,842	3,893	4,256	4,696	4,599	5,084	5,178
Females Total 3	843	865	968	1,010	933	1,126	1,217	1,301	1,374	1,256
Under 21	102	174	247	325	299	307	258	250	224	147
21-30	470	460	475	497	454	531	638	654	717	624
Over 30	271	231	246	188	180	288	321	397	433	485
Community sentence 2	12,320	12,515	12,921	12,366	12,488	13,800	15,939	15,563	17,005	16,481
Males Total 3	10,762	10,775	11,000	10,389	10,633	11,658	13,341	12,969	14,258	13,769
Under 21	4,811	4,505	4,669	4,132	3,997	4,128	4,563	4,082	4,422	4,270
21-30	3,773	3,866	3,884	3,754	3,963	4,469	5,136	5,054	5,461	5,189
Over 30	2,176	2,399	2,444	2,502	2,673	3,059	3,642	3,833	4,374	4,310
Females Total 3	1,558	1,740	1,921	1,977	1,855	2,142	2,598	2,594	2,747	2,712
Under 21	424	459	547	548	544	515	562	518	568	574
21-30	641	727	774	889	795	1,015	1,258	1,150	1,187	1,180
Over 30	492	553	597	539	516	612	777	926	992	958
Financial penalty 2	104,630	103,728	92,548	85,414	71,846	77,483	79,994	86,138	85,016	80,547
Males Total 3	90,728	89,723	81,179	75,019	62,034	67,583	68,395	73,014	71,627	68,463
Under 21	18,293	17,819	16,168	14,841	12,755	14,129	14,108	14,498	13,891	13,782
21-30	36,549	35,597	31,214	27,865	23,076	25,131	24,840	25,995	25,057	23,562
Over 30	34,897	35,380	32,926	31,549	25,571	28,049	29,431	32,517	32,675	31,116
Females Total 3	13,902	14,005	11,369	10,395	9,812	9,900	11,599	13,124	13,389	12,084
Under 21	1,898	1,883	1,669	1,538	1,369	1,330	1,446	1,563	1,498	1,470
21-30	5,468	5,562	4,469	3,867	3,639	3,694	4,040	4,597	4,638	4,146
Over 30	6,132	6,236	4,983	4,742	4,582	4,815	6,110	6,963	7,253	6,468
Other sentence 2	16,896	16,072	15,010	13,852	12,842	13,471	14,157	14,856	15,775	15,096
Males Total 3	12,747	12,147	11,345	10,450	9,527	10,170	10,611	11,023	11,721	11,246
Under 21	4,152	4,183	4,093	3,535	2,957	3,202	3,366	3,253	3,338	3,256
21-30	4,041	3,687	3,293	3,164	3,103	3,312	3,504	3,591	3,627	3,402
Over 30	4,429	4,209	3,918	3,704	3,418	3,642	3,738	4,178	4,756	4,588
Females Total 3	4,149	3,925	3,665	3,402	3,315	3,301	3,546	3,833	4,054	3,850
Under 21	946	924	940	872	750	758	752	732	744	757
21-30	1,511	1,434	1,403	1,253	1,267	1,288	1,372	1,537	1,540	1,452
Over 30	1,499	1,477	1,265	1,265	1,277	1,245	1,422	1,563	1,770	1,641

1. Includes sentence unknown. 2. Excludes persons with sex unknown. 3. Includes persons with age unknown.

Source: Adapted from Scottish Executive (1996, 2007), Criminal Proceedings in Scottish Courts 1996 and 2005/06.

of tools being used corresponds to the fact that 60 cases being considered for an ASBO were rejected in favour of alternative measures (DTZ, 2006).

Formal community-based disposals: a brief overview of use

Formal community-based disposals include Probation Orders, Community Service Orders, Restriction of Liberty Orders, ASBOs and ISMS, all of which were piloted for the adult court and subsequently considered as disposals for the youth justice process in Scotland. The report of the Review of Community Penalties published in November 2007 signalled the Government's intention to legislate for a new version of Community Service Orders. The intention was that the revamped CSO would no longer be a direct alternative to custody and would involve between 20 and 300 hours of unpaid work, would be available to all courts including the JP courts. Recently Kenny MacAskill announced that further funding of £1 million would allow offenders to be put on community service orders more quickly, wanting offenders to pay back to the community by the 'sweat on their brow'. The increase in community sentencing is demonstrated and highlighted in Table 5.2, which illustrates the long-term trend in sentencing decisions in Scotland for all age-categories. Notably, while use of custody has dropped over the time period (from 177,250 in 1986 to 128,089 in 2005/6), community sentences have increased dramatically in usage, from 6,766 in 1986 to 16,481 in 2005/6. In fact, while all other types of sentence have decreased in usage, community sentences have grown year on year, with an increasingly diverse range of sentencing options available.

As Table 5.3 makes clear, this increase in the use of community sentences is across the board.

Table 5.3 Convictions resulting in a community sentence by age and gender: 2000/1– 2004/5

	2000-01	2001-02	2002-03	2003-04	2004-05
All persons(1,2)	12,487	13,800	15,941	15,557	16,952
Under 18	1,385	1,359	1,531	1,481	1,732
18 to 20	3,155	3,284	3,595	3,118	3,240
21 to 25	2,919	3,359	4,016	3,856	3,906
26 to 30	1,839	2,125	2,380	2,344	2,723
31 to 40	2,189	2,530	2,967	3,195	3,541
Over 40	1,000	1,141	1,451	1,563	1,810
Males(2)	10,632	11,658	13,340	12,963	14,215
Females(2)	1,855	2,142	2,598	2,594	2,737

1. Excluding companies and including a small number of convictions where the gender of the offender was not known

2. Includes a small number of convictions where the age of the offender was not known.

Source: Scottish Executive (2006a) Criminal Justice Social Work Statistics, 2005

The Antisocial Behaviour etc (Scotland) Act (2004) provided for the introduction of electronic monitoring for children aged under 16 years, and the courts can now impose an RLO on a young person restricting them to a specific place for up to 12 hours a day in certain prescribed conditions. The Children's Hearings Panel also has the power to impose conditions restricting the movement of a young person when that young person meets the criteria for secure accommodation (i.e. that the young person is likely to abscond and, if so, is likely to be at risk, and is likely to injure him/herself or others). When this occurs, an Intensive Support and Monitoring Service (ISMS), which is a community-based service covering all of the young person's needs, is put in place to support these arrangements. The recent evaluation (Scottish Government, 2008c) of ISMSs claims that the feedback from practitioners has, on the whole, been positive. The findings would also tend to support the view of the last administration that ISMSs have been designed with the welfare needs of the child in mind. However, there have been difficulties in certain areas that lack the resources to provide the necessary programmes to meet the requirements or needs of the child, especially notable with regard to education (Scottish Government, 2008c, para 10.51).

Diversion, mediation and restorative justice

Diversion from prosecution is the referral of an accused to social work or other agencies when it is believed that formal criminal justice proceedings are not necessary (i.e. where there is no overriding public interest for a prosecution). The discretion and decision making rests with the Procurator Fiscal. The Report of the Advisory Group on Youth Crime (Scottish Executive, 2000a) called for a 'greater emphasis on prevention, diversion and the concept of restorative justice including the victim perspective' in its youth justice programme. Policy direction in Scotland is aimed at prevention and early voluntary intervention with compulsion only as a last resort. A range of alternatives to prosecution has therefore been provided, including diversion to social work services, mediation and restorative justice practices. The increased focus on diversionary practices such as restorative justice emanates from the 10 Point Action Plan and National Standards for Youth Justice (Scottish Executive (2006j). Point 6 of the 10 Point Action Plan required the consideration of a Scotland-wide application of a system of cautions/ warnings, and a detailed exploration of restorative cautions, perhaps through piloting. National guidelines on the use of police restorative warnings for young people who offend were issued in June 2004. All police forces now have a mechanism in place to deliver cautions and warnings. The development of the National Standards was part of the 10 Point Action Plan with Objective 2 of the National Standards focusing on improving the range and availability of programmes to stop youth offending.

Restorative justice aims to involve the parties themselves and to some extent the community, although it can be difficult to define what the community represents. In Scotland, restorative justice and restorative practice have evolved essentially in relation to young people. Police restorative warnings are an example, where at an early stage in criminal proceedings suitably trained officers will provide warnings in a 'restorative manner' (Scottish Executive, 2004b). The officer carrying out the warning (the facilitator) is also responsible for ensuring the victim has an input to the warning process, either by arranging the personal attendance of the victim (if the offender has agreed), or by the facilitator's voicing the view of the victim after contacting him or her. In cases where victims are deemed to be especially vulnerable they will be contacted by Victim Support who may also attend at a warning in their place where appropriate. For Scotland there are definitional and conceptual debates. Marshall's definition of restorative justice, for example, defines it as 'a process whereby parties with a stake in a specific offence collectively resolve how to deal with the aftermath of the offence and its implications for the future' (Marshall, 1999).

This suggests that a key element of restorative justice is allowing the parties collective resolution. Focusing on these broader issues extends the scope of restorative approaches being used in many jurisdictions. These approaches seek to involve victims more directly in the process of tackling offending behaviour. The range of measures available can include a focus on victims' issues as part of an intervention programme, requiring the offender to write a letter of apology or, where both parties are willing, bringing the young offender and the victim together to consider the impact of the offence on the victim. Interventions which bring the offender and victim together have been generally well received by all involved, and can help bring home to young offenders the consequences of their actions. The third report of the Home Office independent evaluation of restorative justice schemes in the UK, *Restorative Justice: The Views of Victims and Offenders*, identified some of the views of victims and offenders who took part in restorative justice mediation and conferencing (Shapland *et al.*, 2007). More research into the effectiveness of restorative approaches in helping to reduce levels of further offending among young people would, however, be useful. Introduction of a victim perspective in this way must be undertaken with care and in ways that genuinely promote victims' interests. It will be important to develop protocols and identify best practice in relation to restorative justice approaches.

Conclusion

The statistics presented above show an increase in the use of diversionary activities and community sanctions that reflects the principles underpinning the youth justice process in Scotland. However, it is clear that detention and secure accommodation are still seen as necessary components of the youth justice system. How they should be provided and whether the individual needs of children placed in secure accommodation are being met are questions still open to debate. While ISMSs have been introduced as an alternative to imprisonment and a means of ensuring that the child's needs are fully met it is hard not to see this and other similar developments as signalling yet another shift from the welfarist concerns and ethos of minimal intervention espoused by Kilbrandon, especially as these measures are being implemented in a context of falling crime rates when convictions for young offenders under 21 years are decreasing and offence referrals to the Children's Hearings System are relatively stable.

CHAPTER 6

Young People, Youth Justice and 'Anti-social Behaviour'

Mike Nellis, Kevin Pilkington and Susan Wiltshire

Introduction

Social concern about troublesome behaviour by young people has a long history and 'the antisocial behaviour (ASB) agenda' was one of the ways of reframing the problem and constructing a putative solution (Newburn, 2007b). As discourse, it was associated very specifically with the electoral aspirations and administrative style of the New Labour government that came to power in 1997. The agenda was enacted first in legislation in England, and only later (constituted in a slightly different form) in Scotland. The rhetoric associated with ASB usually denoted a somewhat nebulous, age-unspecific category of people – a problematic *irresponsible minority* disturbing the tranquillity of a conventional *responsible majority* – but it almost always encompassed *young* people. The teenage 'hoodie', singly or in a 'gang', and the 'neighbours from hell' (who can range from unruly children in 'problem families' to cantankerous old people living alone) were arguably its most recognisable folk devils, while the Anti-social Behaviour Order (ASBO) became emblematic, in the media and perhaps in the public mind, of official determination to restore order in disorderly places.

The specific concept of anti-social behaviour, however, had no legal status and its utility to New Labour lay partly in the very imprecision as a signifier;

it was, as Mooney and Young (2006, p. 400) put it, 'a formula for a permanent moral anxiety'. ASB was initially synonymous with disorder and 'incivilities' (offensive and unpleasant behaviour in public) which were manifestly less serious than 'crime' and took in vandalism, school discipline problems, unruly tenants, poor parenting, youth unemployment, binge drinking and gang culture. Some of the behaviour denoted by ASB, however, was already criminal, and, in addition, any breaches of its specific legal interventions – which could be imposed in the first place using only civil standards of evidence – themselves became a criminal offence. As a discourse, the ASB agenda thus blended elements of community safety, public protection and punishment and it was this that New Labour believed would give it electoral appeal. In England and Wales, initially with strong support from the police, the ASB agenda, as it applied to young people, was vigorously implemented and remains important, although the Westminster government subsequently took to calling it 'the respect agenda' (for overviews of the agenda's evolution see Waiton, 2008; Atkinson and Helms, 2007; Squires, 2008). In Scotland, the story has been slightly different.

Community Safety Partnerships involving police, social work and youth, and voluntary and community organisations were tackling many aspects of ASB, without it being called such, before New Labour's agenda emerged. Although ASB was recognised as a serious issue by the Convention of Scottish Local Authorities (COSLA), the precise New Labour agenda was perceived by them as too centrist, and was strongly resisted by both social workers and civil liberty groups, who objected particularly to its unduly coercive elements, and to the blurring of civil and criminal interventions. (It might, sadly, be said of social workers that they did not engage adequately with the community safety agenda, even before ASB initiatives were grafted on to it). Even the Scottish police, who recognised that the ASB policy gave them valuable new powers, worried that extensive use and/or overly robust enforcement of the new measures would alienate the communities they seek to serve, especially young people. Youth justice social work, in particular, argued that the ASB agenda decontextualised problem behaviours from their roots in poverty, disregarded social justice, and underestimated the scale and adequacy of welfare-based initiatives that were already available via the children's Hearing System.

While right to defend these principles, the social work stance tends to underplay the ethnographic and journalistic accounts of transgressive behaviour by young people which plainly showed that disadvantage in some neighbourhoods is compounded by crime and ASB (Campbell, 1993; Davies, 1998; Hanley, 2007). Even Elizabeth Burney (2006, p. vii), a strong critic of the ASB agenda in England, conceded that by the 1990s there was clearly a problem 'with some neighbourhoods where people were living daily with abuse, intimidation and disorder that seriously undermined their quality of life and that of their locality'. She believed that New Labour had 'rightly picked up on failures in dealing with long standing disorders in vulnerable communities' but that punishing 'a few individuals whose behaviour is itself often the consequence of public service failure (or at least exacerbated by it) is manifestly the wrong way to go about it' (Burney, p. 165).

In Scotland in May 2007 the New Labour government was replaced by a Scottish National Party (SNP) government, who won without making law and order a prominent feature of their electoral platform, unprecedentedly for a political party in the UK for several decades. In opposition, the SNP had been decidedly lukewarm towards the anti-social behaviour agenda, in power it was something they recognised that they must address, but on their own terms. A very comprehensive review of the 'national antisocial behaviour strategy' was announced in October 2007, under Fergus Ewing, the Minister for Community Safety, with a view to reporting in December 2008.[1] It engaged in a major consultation with established interest groups, as well as the newer ones created by the ASB agenda, e.g. the Antisocial Behaviour Officers' Forum (ASBOF) and the Antisocial Behaviour Lawyers' Forum. It also consulted with young people themselves, via focus groups and blogs, and made timely use of the various evaluations of New Labour's ASB measures, which were published in the course of 2007.

This chapter will consider these developments, tracing the origin and implementation of the ASB agenda in Scotland as it affects young people. It will focus primarily on the flagship legal measures, using the recent evaluative data, and, with an eye on the Ewing Review, it will suggest that the emerging concept of 'community justice' may enable a genuinely constructive rapprochement between those who champion the primacy of young people's welfare and those who, for no less progressive reasons, insist that the immediate safety needs of people in disadvantaged communities have been neglected for too long and must now be met.

The emergence of the anti-social behaviour agenda

Although associated with New Labour, the previous Conservative government had laid the foundation of what became the anti-social behaviour agenda via its interest in the 'broken windows' thesis. This underpinned both the emergence of zero tolerance policing and the idea of community safety (Wilson and Kelling, 1982). The New Labour slogan 'tough on crime and tough on the causes of crime', which articulated the demands of respectable working class communities, laid the foundations of it. Explicit interest in the political philosophy of communitarianism, with its insistence that civic rights could only be enjoyed if civic responsibilities were also fulfilled, was short-lived but traces of its influence live on (which can be reworked to more positive effect). There was also a strongly managerial influence on the agenda, insofar as it sought a more meticulous regulation of behaviour in the community than had hitherto been considered legitimate, desirable or possible (Blunkett, 2001). The first wave of policy was implemented in the Crime and Disorder Act 1998, the second in the Antisocial Behaviour Act 2003, which was based on a White Paper *Respect and Responsibility – Taking a Stand against Anti- Social Behaviour* (Home Office, 2003). It fore-grounded tough talk and coercive measures, but surreptitiously added an underpinning of social inclusion measures.

Putting Our Communities First (Scottish Executive, 2003b) was the key White Paper in Scotland. It proposed a range of new measures: ASBOs for under-16s, dispersal orders, Parenting Orders, closure orders, fixed penalties for noise nuisance, intensive supervision programmes (including electronic tagging) and the use of voluntary Acceptable Behaviour Contracts. A consultation on these proposals confirmed that some already disadvantaged Scottish communities felt particularly blighted by ASB (and crime) and wanted effective action taken. There was strong support for increasing protection for victims and witnesses of ASB, less for introducing electronic monitoring for under-16s and for Parenting Orders (Flint *et al.*, 2003). The Antisocial Behaviour etc (Scotland) Act was implemented in June 2004. The then First Minister characterised it as a crackdown on 'ned culture' and as a means of making life more tolerable for disadvantaged communities. The media were enlisted by the Executive to publicise the strategy and, because it played directly into tabloid sentiments (and to some extent had been shaped by them), some newspapers became independent supporters of it. The Glasgow *Evening Times* (19 January 2007), for example, clearly admired 'anti-ned' dispersal orders and campaigned for them to be set in place permanently, beyond their initial three months.

The focus was never simply on young people. Parenting, alleged decline in the quality of which can always be used as a potent symbol of social decline, was equally central. While there is room for argument about what constitutes good and bad parenting, there is clear evidence that parental neglect, indifference and inconsistency contribute to delinquency, that these can be sustained over generations, and that good parenting skills are hard to acquire and uphold in conditions of poverty and disadvantage. It is less clear that threatening parents with fines and imprisonment if they do not attend parenting classes – a cornerstone of the ASB agenda – is an acceptable or sensible way forward.

Implementing the anti-social behaviour agenda

We noted above that many of the issues clustered together under the rubric of ASB were receiving separate attention from a range of agencies. To fully understand what the implementation of the ASB agenda meant requires a distinction between the implementation of the 'core' measures in the 2004 legislation, and the broader set of responses to disorderly behaviour in particular settings (such as schools) which proceeded alongside them, and which were likely to outlast their association with the discourse of ASB.

New Labour presented the measures in the 2004 legislation as something which, if placed at the forefront of local ASB strategies, would make a rapid difference to community safety. The police and local authority view, however, was that the measures were more of a back-stop and hoped in many instances never to use them. This created tensions between local and central government, forcing the latter to undertake a protracted campaign to win legitimacy for the new measures and sometimes threatening to withdraw funding if the powers were ignored. It initiated media coverage through TV, radio and posters that encouraged people to report anti-social behaviour, simultaneously accompanied by ASBO roadshows in a number of towns and cities. A Standing-Up to Anti-Social Behaviour Award scheme, sponsored by the Co-op, highlighted the courage and commitment of citizens – to date, community wardens, youth workers and a teacher – who challenged bad behaviour in particular local communities (see www.antisocialbehaviourscotland.com).

The government organised trips to Manchester for journalists and local councillors to showcase the attractions of junior ASBOs. This rarely led to changes in local authority behaviour. In the run-up to the May 2007 election, Labour's manifesto reaffirmed the importance of the ASB agenda and stated that the party would introduce the 'naming and shaming' of individuals, including juveniles, who cause distress to local communities (a Mancunian practice). The Labour leader of Edinburgh city council, who promptly questioned the value of this, typified the ongoing central–local clash over ASB. The following summaries of how the core measures in the legislation had fared up to April 2007 are mostly taken from evaluations commissioned by the then Scottish Executive.

Local authority anti-social behaviour strategies

The 2004 Act required police and local authorities to draw up ASB strategies for their areas. Flint *et al.* (2007) undertook in-depth case studies of these in four local authorities between March 2006 and March 2007, concluding that while enhanced partnership working did occur, based on PIER (prevention, intervention, enforcement and rehabilitation) principles, there were no marked reductions in ASB, possibly because the initiatives were at an early stage of development. Numbers of reported incidents actually rose, probably because of the availability of new services to deal with them, but in many instances ASB remained underreported, sometimes because of fear of intimidation, making victim and witness support services all the more important. Methods of intervention varied in different local authorities and in neighbourhoods within them, ranging from community wardens, concierges, mediation services, night noise services, a freephone anti-social behaviour hotline, increased use of mobile CCTV and a family support project; initiatives to tackle underage drinking were particularly valued by residents. A separate evaluation of community wardens, introduced nationwide by the Executive under the Building Strong, Safe, Attractive Communities initiative in March 2003, indicated that while police found them useful as sources of intelligence and witness support, it was difficult to prove that their presence reduced crime (Hayton *et al.*, 2007). Not all instances of ASB were in deprived areas: prearranged fights between rival groups of youngsters after school ended were quelled using mounted police patrols, backed up by foot patrols, in Stamperland, a middle-class area in East Renfrewshire (*Glasgow Evening Times*, 16 March 2006).

It is in the context of general ASB strategies that Acceptable Behaviour Contracts (ABCs) should be mentioned. These are written contracts between a person who has engaged in anti-social behaviour and a range of local statutory and voluntary agencies, including registered social landlords. The contract specifies the behaviour concerned, requires the perpetrator to stop (and enlists his or consent to do so) and sets out the consequences of breach, usually an ASBO or (in the case of adult tenants) a possession order. It was hoped that ABCs would nip ASB in the bud, before it became more serious (Pawson and McKenzie, 2006). In 2005/6, 27 of the 32 local authorities used ABCs at least once, 41 organisations had used them, and 75% were not breached in a 12-month period.

ASBOs

ASBOs were the one element of the 'English' Crime and Disorder Act 1998 (s 19) that were introduced into Scotland.[2] Local authorities, and later registered social landlords, including housing associations, were to apply for them through Sheriff Courts. They were primarily intended as an alternative to eviction, although other uses were envisaged (Dewar and Payne, 2003). Antisocial Behaviour Orders for 12- to 15-year-olds were introduced in 2004. Sheriffs must be satisfied that the Order is needed to protect another person, and all other measures have been tried, and arrange a Children's Hearing to ascertain these things. Although breach is a criminal offence, imprisonment cannot be considered as a penalty, although secure accommodation can. Formally, the four local authorities studied by DTZ were committed to using ASBOs on young people, but there was tension between different departments within them; in the event, over a three-year implementation period only 3% were made on under-16s, with 74% on over-21s, and 21% on 16- to 21-year-olds (DTZ and Heriot-Watt University, 2007, p. 48). One local government official noted 'a particularly weak relationship between ASB strategy and the Youth Justice strategy in his area'. Another was quoted as saying: 'There can be a mutual lack of understanding between Social Work and Housing or Community Safety. However, relationships at an operational level have improved significantly in recent years' (DTZ and Heriot-Watt University, 2007, p. 35).

In 2005/6, 96 young people were considered for ASBOs but only four were granted on 12- to 15-year-olds, two in Edinburgh, one in Dundee, and one in Renfrewshire. Most cases were resolved in other ways. An unspecified number of young people were made subject to ASBOs when informal solutions, such as ABCs, broke down, but after they had become 16. 'There is no sign at the moment of the pattern of ASBO use resembling that in England and Wales, where more than one third of orders are made against persons under 16' (DTZ and Heriot-Watt University, 2007, p. 35).

Dispersal Orders

These enable police to disperse two or more people from a specified area. The penalties for breaching a Dispersal Order are a fine of up to £2500 or custody up to 3 months. Fourteen orders in 11 places were granted such an order by April 2007, all targeted on young people (Cavanagh, 2007). The first was made in Mid Calder (12 miles west of Edinburgh) where teenagers were banned from congregating after dark at weekends. The other places were Aberdeen, Dennistoun, Dingwall, Dumfries (2), Edinburgh, Knightswood, Lockerbie, Moffat and Sauchie. There were substantial reductions in ASB during the three-month periods the orders were in force, and much satisfaction among local residents as to the respite this afforded. Police forces too found the powers useful, a proactive improvement on previous means of dealing with clusters of young people engaging in ASB, without any serious displacement of ASB to other places. Alcohol misuse, fighting, late-night noise, shouting, swearing, urination and vandalism were the main behaviours concerned. Overall, once orders were made, the police issued directions to disperse on 867 occasions. Thirty-eight arrests for breach were made, 5 on juveniles – though the only proven breaches appear to have been by adults. Some areas experienced reductions in ASB beyond the three months the Dispersal Order pertained, while in others ASB returned to pre-order levels. The difference is explicable in terms of the introduction of diversionary activities and problem solving – mediation, sharing of information by police, local authorities and other agencies, and targeting of perpetrators – in the former. There was a sense among residents that more could be done in this respect, although young people in dispersal zones felt discriminated against.

The police were legally required to consult with the local authority before seeking authorisation for dispersal, and in most instances were painstaking in doing so. In one instance where they authorised it, the local authority had not supported the arrangement, fearing, in the police view, that it would pressure their youth justice services to provide diversionary activities. In addition, there were tensions

> between different council departments. Some social work and youth services representatives ... were concerned about balancing the needs of the perpetrators of Anti-Social behaviour with the need to protect the public from harassment. This often provoked tension between council, social work and community safety departments who often assisted the police. In one location youth justice workers and social

work officers were worried that young people might be criminalised with the use of the powers. It was agreed in the procedures that these departments would be alerted at an early stage if there was a breach for an under16 year old or if there were other concerns, so that it could be channelled through a children's Hearing. (Cavanagh, 2007, p. 44)

Criteria for taking dispersal powers are more stringent in Scotland than England, resulting in proportionately fewer orders. The cost of each zone varied between £5000 and £7500 and they required intensive use of police resources. Costs prohibited the creation of some dispersal zones that might otherwise have been set up, but the police have traditionally had strategies for dealing with high crime hotspots without resorting to dispersal. High-profile patrolling can reassure and speed up response times; mobile CCTV and plain clothes officers can be used to gather evidence. These measures can be used instead of, or as part of, dispersal orders.

Noise abatement

The Local Authority Antisocial Neighbour Noise Nuisance Services established by the 2004 Act were not specifically targeted at young people, but a residents' survey undertaken by DTZ Consulting and Research (2007) in eight sample local authorities showed that teenagers and substance misusers were perceived to be the main source of noise. Whoever they are, half of noisemakers have no sympathy with complaining neighbours. Only 13% of residents experienced noise as a major problem, mostly in poorly insulated rented accommodation in disadvantaged areas, but of these almost half said they would not report it, fearing intimidation by the perpetrators or doubting that any agency would do anything. The availability of noise nuisance services when DTZ undertook its evaluation in 2005/6 was limited, but experience suggested that either informal mediation between complainants and noisemakers or fixed penalty notices for the more recalcitrant were the best means of resolving the issue, although there was some evidence that fine enforcement was lax.

Parenting Orders

Symbolically, Parenting Orders – compulsory instruction in parenting skills for up to twelve months – were an important element in the ASB legislation, but substantively they proved to be the least used, perhaps the least needed – and the least compatible with Kilbrandon principles.[3] The Scottish Executive consulted carefully on them, recognised continued scepticism about them among social workers, Children's Panel members and voluntary childcare organisations and accepted that they should be used only when all else has failed. Concerns about the very principle of coercing parents to seek help, its compatibility with welfare legislation, availability of resources, and the consequences for children of parents' breaching the order remained. The Executive set up a 3-year national pilot in April 2005, and issued guidance to Reporters, local authorities and Children's Hearings. Aberlour Childcare Trust Parenting Development Project was commissioned by the Executive to produce a national framework document on Parenting Orders. It already had a successful track record of engaging with anti-social parents without resort to legal coercion, as did NCH's Dundee Families Project (Scott, 2006). Local authorities proved lax in developing their protocols in respect of Parenting Orders, with some indicating that ASBOs were a more preferable response to an anti-social young person than an order directed at their parents (Walters and Woodward, 2007). The upshot of such ingrained scepticism, coupled with the availability of non-coercive measures that achieved the same ends, was that by April 2007 no Parenting Orders had been made at all. This contrasts sharply with England, where 766 were made between October 2003 and September 2005.

Schools, educational support and early intervention

In this section we explore an aspect of disruptive youth behaviour that is both within and without the prevailing discourse of ASB, the proposed solutions to which will arguably outlast the particular concerns and formulations of New Labour. Schools are understood to be central to breaking the cycle of violence – the Violence Reduction Unit, for example, has distributed leaflets on good parenting to all Scotland's primary schools, and police officers routinely visit schools to speak about the consequences of criminal behaviour. Nonetheless, debates about, and initiatives in respect of, school discipline tend to proceed independently of it. Widespread concern is persistently being expressed by teaching associations and unions, who relate the issue of disruption to class size and educational policy more generally. School exclusions are usually taken as an indicator of the problem. Scottish Executive figures in January 2007 showed an 18% increase in exclusions over four years. There were 42,990 cases of exclusion (involving 22,500 pupils, some being excluded more than once) from primary and secondary schools in 2005–6. The average was 226 on any school day. Most pupils were sent home for persistent disobedience and some for verbal abuse, but 30 per day were sent home for assault, and 20 for fighting. Alcohol misuse was a factor in exclusion. Policy statements invariably emphasise the routine good behaviour of most Scottish pupils, identifying a problem with the minority. The use of classroom assistants and special needs auxiliaries are usually presented as ways of reducing exclusions. School culture is important, and exclusions are possibly associated with attainment cultures rather than more rounded approaches to children's wellbeing. There are clear links between deprivation and school exclusion, with significantly higher rates in poorer areas of Glasgow and West Dunbartonshire.

Increasingly younger age groups are being drawn into the ASB agenda, including pre-schoolers and (rhetorically, at least) unborn babies. This may not have been what New Labour *originally* had in mind, but as doctors, psychologists and pharmaceutical companies have begun to re-affirm the biological correlates of anti-social behaviour and the importance of early intervention, they have proved willing to encompass it. While there clearly are health dimensions to bringing up children, the press have latched rather uncritically onto claims that medicine may have a significant part to play in reducing future anti-social behaviour, as indicated by the following headlines: 'Unloved babies become anti-social adults' (*The Scotsman*, 26 November 2005), 'Tests to reveal ASBO babies' (*The Scotsman*, 28 September 2006) and 'Blair to target the ASBO babies' (*London Evening Standard*, 2 April 2007). At the heart of the issue is the emergence of an apparently new syndrome linked to anti-social behaviour, Attention Deficit Hyperactivity Disorder (ADHD). This has been defined as 'developmentally inappropriate inattention and impassivity, with or without hyperactivity', and is diagnosed four times more frequently in boys than girls. Response to this diagnosis is usually medication, in particular Ritalin, prescriptions for which have doubled in the last decade. There are complex issues at stake here. While biological contributions to behaviour (anti-social or otherwise) cannot be discounted, medicalisation can be used as a strategy for producing docility in people who have been deemed unduly disruptive of organisational requirements in schools, nurseries and, indeed, families. One should clearly not hold young people responsible for behaviour that has genuine medical causes, but equally one should not medicalise behaviour that has social or domestic causes, and thereby deflect attention from addressing social causes. Although some middle-class parents may take comfort from an ADHD diagnosis – one's child's behaviour is not 'wilfully bad' after all – it will arguably be the infant children of the poor who are most subject to the new medicalisation, alongside the more punitive strategies targeted on their older brothers and sisters. There are huge risks of stigma and labelling with early intervention conceived in this way.

Conclusion

By conflating the idea that welfare measures are good in themselves with the idea that they are morally superior at all times to all other interventions, youth justice social work has turned a blind eye to the debilitating consequences of ASB in poor neighbourhoods (despite past invitations to consider broader 'quality of life' issues (Seed and Lloyd, 1997), which are in any case at the heart of the Community Planning infrastructure introduced in Scotland in 2003. Community Safety Partnerships, and some of the specific ASB teams set up in local authorities, have understood this better – even when pressured by New Labour to respond in simplistic ways. There are undeniably dangers in the untrammelled use of merely coercive measures to create safety (or at least a semblance of it), but for youth justice to repudiate them 'in principle' is to deny any kind of relief to already disadvantaged communities that are blighted by criminal and anti-social behaviour. Given the overarching emphasis on partnership in Scotland's Community Planning strategy, a synthesis of the two positions ought to be possible. On the eve of the SNP victory, Scotland's leading liberal newspaper seemed to believe so, embracing the new powers in moderation, and questioning over-reliance on traditional social work approaches:

> Councils whose residents are suffering disproportionally from youth crime have been among those granting markedly fewer orders than elsewhere. Glasgow City Council, for example, took the view that intervening to prevent youth crime was more effective than using the Executive's sanctions. Both sides in this argument have some merit. (*The Herald*, editorial, 21 April 2007)

The impetuousness with which New Labour promoted its ASB agenda alienated social work and underplayed the value of grassroots community organisations such as FARE, set up in 1989 in Easterhouse to improve the quality of life of its residents, and Calton Athletic, a football team run by and for ex-drug users (Holman, 1997; Bryce, 2005). Without ever conceptualising anti-social behaviour as such, this type of organisation makes vital, supportive interventions in the lives of young people, families and communities. But even FARE's director has conceded that Easterhouse's enduring, territorially based gangs restrict the free movement of non-members through adjoining neighbourhoods, undermining their quality of life and socialising youngsters into violent lifestyles (*The Sunday Herald*, 15 July 2007). Once one has factored serious violence into the mix, the argument that coercive powers are excessive does not seem so weak – not as a stand-alone punitive measure but as an adjunct to preventive and diversionary activities with longer-term social goals. Official agencies should undoubtedly foster community tolerance towards mere youthful exuberance, but potential victims of violence – who may be young people themselves – must be spared intimidation and harm. While New Labour might have been better advised to strengthen existing Community Safety Partnerships, they were not wholly mistaken in giving local authorities extra powers to deal with ASB – while local authorities were quite right to use them in moderation and to integrate them with what they were already doing.

The SNP government quickly abandoned the strident language used by New Labour to promote its agenda, and eased the pressure on local authorities to make more use of the legislative measures. Fergus Ewing's Review signalled a change of emphasis from the outset, recognising the fundamental importance of exploring 'the balance between prevention, intervention, enforcement and rehabilitation', the need to foster 'community engagement', to facilitate 'integrated service provision' and to develop a sensible 'media and communication' strategy (which implies an appropriate vocabulary and narrative) that engages the Scottish public. Beyond this, little has been indicated about the likely direction of its thinking, although Ewing has incorporated the use of fixed penalty notices as a response to ASB into its agenda, in the light of existing evidence as to its relevance (Eberst and Staines, 2006; Ewing Review, 2007; 2008). The breadth of this Review's remit, its commitment to consensus and its strategic ambition augurs well for the production of a somewhat more sophisticated vision than that of New Labour. The tone of the subsequent Report, which appeared on the Scottish Government website in March 2009, does indeed break away from the emphasis on the previous government's anti-social behaviour agenda.

Given the Review's attention to 'integrated service provision', the concept of 'community justice' – which has already entered the vocabulary of Scottish governance, without much attention having yet been paid to its practical implications – may provide that narrative. Its theorists emphasise the importance of *blending* strategies for supervising offenders in the community with strategies for creating safer communities, rather than seeing these as philosophically, administratively or professionally separate fields (Nellis, 2000; Karp and Clear, 2002; Williams, 2005). It is in fact an apt term for much of the progressive work *which already goes on* in the presently separate spheres of young offender supervision and community safety, and it is to be hoped that Scotland's eight regional Community Justice Authorities will finally break down these silos and foster the emergence of a new cluster of professionals who see community justice as an integrated field of work. The philosophy is grounded in a radical communitarian rather than a liberal understanding of social order, which emphasises interdependence and mutual obligations rather than the rights of any one group, even unruly children, over another (Hughes, 1998). It is oriented towards informal and local solutions, rather than legal and penal ones, giving due weight to welfare and restorative interventions but allowing for coercion as a necessary measure of last resort in the interest of a greater communal good (see Hill *et al.*, 2007b, p. 17, and Crawford and Newburn, 2003, on the limitations of restorative justice).

The ongoing developmental work of Community Safety Partnerships and the internal dialogue stimulated between local authority departments (notably youth justice social work, housing and community safety) as a result of the ASB agenda itself need to continue, within a framework set by Fergus Ewing's Report. DTZ's evidence indicates that inter-professional dialogue on ASB was often fraught but, as David Prior's (2007) research in England shows, there are already affinities in the way different departments work, a marked preference for informalism for example, which offer grounds for believing that common understandings may become easier in future. Youth justice social workers were understandably sceptical of the ASB agenda when it was pushed by central government as something self-evidently superior to prevailing interventions, without any respect for their ethos, or for existing work in community safety, but a climate is now emerging in which the more rounded claims of community justice might legitimately be considered as a way forward.

Notes

1 The Report Promoting Positive Outcomes: working together to prevent anti-social behaviour appeared on the Scottish Government's website in March 2009.
2 In the course of Scottish parliamentary debate on the ASB Bill some legal constraints on the flagship orders were introduced that did not exist in England. Some differences

in the substance of the ASB agenda in England and Wales simply reflected a time-lag in the implementation of different measures in the two countries. In England the electronic monitoring of juveniles and the reduction of persistent offending had been implemented before the ASB legislation was passed: in Scotland, simply because they were implemented later, both were incorporated into the ASB agenda.

3 The Kilbrandon Report was emphatic in its opposition to coercing parents: 'It is intended, wherever possible, not to supersede the natural beneficial influences of the home and the family, but wherever possible to strengthen, support and supplement them. .... coercive powers in relation to parents of juvenile delinquents .... are ultimately incompatible with the nature of the education process itself, more particularly in the context of the parent child relationship' (1964, para 35).

CHAPTER 7

The Future of Youth Justice?

Michele Burman and Jenny Johnstone

Kilbrandon legacy

As the preceding chapters have shown, the youth justice landscape in Scotland has undergone considerable expansion and change, particularly in the years since devolution. The debate about youth justice has become increasingly – and rather unhelpfully – polarised between welfare and punishment, needs and deeds, victims and offenders.

Yet much of the Scottish system's distinctiveness remains. The Children's Hearings System still lies at the heart of the youth justice system in Scotland. Most young people up to age 16 years (and some up to 18 years) who offend continue to be dealt with in the Hearings System, which retains a commitment to the paramountcy principle. As we have seen, the System is increasingly taking on characteristics of the adult criminal justice system. Nevertheless, there is evidence of continued support, apparent in some aspects of youth justice policy and practice discourse, for several of the core elements of the Kilbrandon welfarist ethos that underpins the Hearings System, most notably:

- that children who offend and those in need of care and protection have similar needs and that a holistic, social educational model of intervention is likely to be the most effective means of addressing such needs;
- that decisions should be made in the *best interests* of the child;
- the recognition of the importance of early intervention for those identified as being most at risk as a means of nipping offending behaviour in the bud;

- the continued separation of adjudication (which comes under the remit of the Reporter or, in cases where grounds for referral are disputed, the courts) from disposition (which comes under the remit of the Hearing).

Taken together, adherence to these basic tenets, along with the recognition of the importance of community involvement in the Hearings System and the emphasis on informal procedures that maximise participation of children and their families in decision making, serve to distinguish the Scottish youth justice system from other European jurisdictions, and also provide some protection from the encroachment of the more punitive practices found south of the border.

That said, there have been a number of challenges to the Kilbrandon ethos. Perhaps most significant of these are the incursion of the risk principle, through the Children (Scotland) Act 1995, which enabled the Hearings System to place the principle of public protection above that of the child's best interests in cases where the child presents a significant risk to the public. There is also the gradual (but not so subtle) elision that has taken place between the community safety and youth justice agendas, marking a clear shift from a child-centred focus to a focus on the concerns of neighbourhoods and victims. The water-shed *Action Plan to Reduce Youth Crime* (2002b) introduced an emphasis on persistent offending, the development and expansion of programmes based on 'what works' principles (focused on criminogenic needs rather than welfare-based needs), and the increasing emphasis on victims as stakeholders. Soon after, the introduction of the contentious anti-social behaviour legislation introduced electronic monitoring and the potential for criminalisation of parents (where the proposed Parenting Orders are breached). In the face of such developments, and the implementation of more targeted youth justice measures, the philosophy of the Kilbrandon approach is becoming diluted. Although the Hearings System continues to be seen as a successful mechanism for taking many young people under the age of 16 out of the adult criminal justice system (with no apparent adverse effects on levels of youth offending) the dominance of welfarism within Scottish youth justice has markedly diminished.

Recent years have witnessed a new era of youth justice in Scotland, one that is underpinned by a complex set of rationales that much of the time locate the interests of society above the interests of the child. Political rhetoric and a range of policy initiatives in recent years also show evidence of shifting from a concern with the social and personal needs of young offenders to incorporate more of a focus on the nature and frequency of their offences – a focus on deeds rather than needs. The growing punitive approach taken towards young offenders in Scotland, the emphasis on persistent offending and the inception of the Youth Court, the 'toughening-up' of sanctions, the development and expansion of programmes based on 'what works' principles, and the renewed focus on risk assessment and surveillance taken together risk eroding the very important distinction between youth justice and adult criminal justice that Kilbrandon so strongly underscored.

Future directions, future challenges?

Criminalisation

Kilbrandon recognised the negative consequences for young people of early criminalisation. There is now a well-established body of research evidence outlining the negative effects of prosecution for young people, the adverse consequences that follow from their involvement in the criminal justice system, and the limited deterrent effect that it has for preventing re-offending among this group (see, for example, Tonry and Doob, 2004; McAra and McVie, 2007).

The age of criminal responsibility is an integral part of Scots law. Currently, Scotland has one of the lowest ages (8 years) of criminal responsibility in the world. Not only is this somewhat at odds with the age points at which children gain capacity in other areas of Scots law, it is considered by many academic and political commentators to be too low. Indeed, the Cabinet Secretary for Justice, Kenny MacAskill, publicly declared in early 2009 that: 'There is no good reason for Scotland to continue to have the lowest age of criminal responsibility in Europe. Most importantly the evidence shows that prosecution at an early age increases the chance of reoffending.' The low age of criminal responsibility also runs contrary to international standards. In 2007, the UN Committee monitoring compliance with the UNCRC published a General Comment that the minimum acceptable age at which children should be held accountable for their actions before full (adult) criminal justice proceedings should not be lower than 12 years in any member state. The shift towards a higher age of criminal age of responsibility in Scotland could be viewed as demonstrating confidence in the Children's Hearings System in dealing with young people under the age of 12. The Bill can also be seen as an attempt to demonstrate adherence to international principles and standards, and bring Scots law more into line with jurisdictions across Europe. The introduction of the restriction on prosecution of those under 12 years also implements the main recommendations of the Scottish Law Commission's report (*Report on Age of Criminal*

Responsibility, 2002), yet falls short of the recommendation to abolish the existing conclusive presumption in relation to under-8-year-olds. In essence, the Bill proposes that 8 years would be retained as the age below which children are deemed incapable of committing crime; 12 would be introduced as the age below which children are immune to prosecution and 16 would remain as the (usual) age of automatic referral to the adult justice system. Another way of reading the Bill might be to suggest that there may be grounds here for arguing that the debate about raising the age of criminal responsibility is evidence of a re-assertion of welfarist values. Yet what is proposed is not quite the same as decriminalisation of those under 12; rather it confers immunity from prosecution for 8- to 11-year-olds. This seems overly complicated, and a more strongly welfarist approach might be to completely decriminalise up to the age of 12 and introduce a new ground of referral for the Children's Hearing of what would otherwise be an offence but for the person's age.

Transition between youth and adult systems – a narrowing gap

A key concern for some time in Scotland has been the transition of young people from the youth to the adult criminal justice systems. Poor information-sharing and joint working across the systems have been identified as key weaknesses, but the underlying concern is the rapidity (and inevitability) with which many young people find themselves out of the Hearings System and into prison. Scotland's incarceration rates – of all age groups – attract censure. Scotland is the only UK jurisdiction that routinely deals with young people aged 16–17 years in the adult criminal courts, and incarceration rates for this group are high. This reality sits very uneasily with any commitment to the decriminalisation of young people.

Proposals under the Criminal Justice and Licensing (Scotland) Bill will, if successful, abolish the legislation that allows 14- and 15-year-olds to be remanded to adult prisons, and Scottish Ministers have publicly committed to place all sentenced under-16-year-olds in secure accommodation (rather than prison) and, wherever possible, retain them there until they reach 18 years. *Scotland's Choice*, the recent report by the Prisons Commission (2008), recommended a specialist Hearing for 16- and 17-year-olds, with the objective of reducing the numbers of young people sent to prison. It remains to be seen whether the Government, despite its publicly stated commitment to end the practice of sending under-16-year-olds to prison articulated in *Protecting Scotland's Communities: Fair Fast and Flexible Justice* (Scottish Government, 2008h), will implement this recommendation.

There is therefore a stated political will to retain young offenders in the community for as long as is feasible. But what is feasible? Whyte (2009) draws attention to the numerous structural barriers to diversion for young people, and the range of financial, practical and logistical disincentives for local authorities to attempt to retain very troublesome youth beyond the age of 16 years within the Hearings System. The financial costs of secure accommodation and the intensive support of young people within the community falls within their budget, whereas prosecution, custody, and probation costs are met centrally. This situation tends to encourage early discharge from the Hearings System for the most challenging youth (Whyte, 2009, pp. 202–3), who are quickly – and somewhat inevitably – drawn into the adult system.

While those working within the Hearing System recognise the distance between the System and the adult criminal justice process, there is little doubt that recent developments risk eroding the distinction between the youth and adult systems. For many, the Youth Court in particular, with its emphasis on fast tracking and the need for speed and efficiency, signals a worrying convergence (an evaluation of the Youth Courts is expected in 2009). Several chapters in this book claim that the Hearing System is at a critical juncture – a stage at which it needs to review and reflect on whether the System and its attendant processes are justified in the current form. There are recurrent concerns about resourcing, and recruitment of lay members. Recent years have seen reviews of the principles and objectives of the Children's Hearings System: 2004 saw the publication of *Getting it Right for Every Child*, and in 2008 *Strengthening for the Future (Scottish Government, 2008k)* recommended the creation of a new national body, the Scottish Children's Hearings Tribunal (SCHT), to oversee the 32 Hearings Panels and deliver training and recruitment services. The *Strengthening for the Future (Scottish Government, 2008k)* consultation included plans to create a single national body bringing together the Children's Reporter service, and the delivery and administration of Children's Hearings as well as assisting the work of the Safeguarders.[1]

At the same time, some of the formal disposals of the System have become progressively more punitive. The Hearing Panel decides whether compulsory measures are required and whether the child should be supervised at home or away from their home environment. The move towards a more formal, tribunal approach illustrates a move towards the more formal characteristics of the adult system.

Risk assessment and risk management

There is a consensus in the international research literature, confirmed by professionals in the field, about the risk factors that predispose young people to offending behaviour, about the most effective ways of counteracting those risk factors, and about the most effective ways of dealing with those who have started offending (Newburn, 2007b). As a result of a combination of emerging evidence about the principles of effective practice and of increasing concern with public protection, the risk of re-offending (or recidivism) and risk of serious harm (to potential victims) have become ever more significant issues in youth justice. While there is continuing reluctance on the part of many youth justice practitioners to embrace risk assessment techniques (Burman *et al.*, 2007), and despite a lack of robust validation evidence, the use of actuarial risk assessment tools for assessing young people at risk of offending and re-offending is officially endorsed in Scotland. With the publication in 2008 by the Scottish Government of *Preventing Offending by Young People: A Framework for Action* a key emphasis is squarely on the early identification of young people at risk of offending and the management of that risk. The Report exhorts that agencies should focus on the identification, assessment, planning and management of this group of children and young people (2008g, p. 11). There is a growing tendency in the risk management of children and young people who offend to deploy a range of interventions that seek to address both the needs of the young person as well as the interest of the public in protection from danger (Burman *et al.*, 2007; Scottish Government, 2008e). This is echoed in the aforementioned Report (2008, p. 12) and those working with this group are asked to take into account both the *needs* and *risks* of a high-risk child or young person. This raises key questions not only about the adoption of a risk-based agenda for youth justice, but about the practical and ideological challenges it may pose for those who work within it.

Responsibilisation

Along with an emphasis on the identification and management of risk posed by young people, Scotland has also witnessed increased emphasis on the responsibilisation of individual young people, their parents and, as evidenced by the recent Government publication on youth offending (Scottish Government, 2008g), the community within which the young person resides. Part of this focus is the development of youth citizenship and engagement strategies, which, along with the concept of responsibilisation, can be seen as attempting to positively engage with young people. For example, following a National Youth

Summit on Alcohol held by Scottish Government in 2008, it was announced that the National Youth Commission was to carry out an investigation into Scotland's relationship to alcohol and, in particular, its impact on young people. This dovetails with key government national outcomes and performance indicators, specifically tackling inequality, building communities responsible for their own environment, and opportunities for young people to develop as active learners and responsible citizens. However, a flip side of such strategies is the potential they have for placing an undue burden on young people to effectively police their communities and peer groups.

Developments in Community Justice

This book has highlighted that 'engagement' and 'active citizenship' strategies can be seen on various levels: at a local level through Community Planning Partnerships; at a national level as evidenced by the Ewing Review (2008) and subsequent Report (Scottish Government, 2009b), as well as on a strategic European level. The European Commission Paper *New Impetus for European Youth* (Commission of the European Communities, 2001) sets out key targets for member states to achieve. These include: 'listening and offering a forum for local initiatives' (2001, p. 5); 'developing autonomy for young people' and 'participation primarily in the local community' (2001, p. 16); 'volunteering as social participation' (2001, p. 17); 'real rather than symbolic participation' (2001, p. 26). Taken together, these both recognise and foreground wider forms of youth participation other than in schools or colleges, and aim at transferability of skills and development – employability, social protection, social participation and active citizenship.

The Ewing Report (Scottish Government, 2009b) recognised the fundamental importance of exploring 'the balance between prevention, intervention, enforcement and rehabilitation', the need to foster 'community engagement', to facilitate 'integrated service provision' and to develop a sensible 'media and communication' strategy (implying an appropriate vocabulary and narrative) that engages the Scottish public. Beyond this, little has been indicated about the likely direction of its thinking, although Ewing has incorporated the use of fixed penalty notices as a response to anti-social behaviour into its agenda, in the light of existing evidence as to its relevance (Eberst and Staines, 2006; Ewing Review 2007; 2008). The breadth of this Review's remit and the tone of the subsequent Report, with its commitment to consensus and its strategic ambition, augurs well for the production of a somewhat more sophisticated vision than that of earlier administrations.

The ongoing developmental work of Community Safety Partnerships and the internal dialogue stimulated between local authority departments (notably youth justice social work, housing and community safety) resulting from the anti-social behaviour agenda look likely to continue, within a framework set by the Ewing Report (Scottish Government, 2009b). While Scottish research (DTZ Pieda, 2005) indicates that inter-professional dialogue on anti-social behaviour can be fraught, research carried out in England reveals affinities in the way different departments work. A marked preference for informalism, for example, offers grounds for believing that common understandings may become easier in future. Youth justice social workers in Scotland were initially – and perhaps understandably – sceptical of the anti-social behaviour agenda when it was rationalised by central government as something self-evidently superior to prevailing interventions, without any respect for their ethos, or for existing work in community safety. However, a climate seems now to be emerging in which the more rounded claims of *community justice* might legitimately be considered as a way forward in Scotland.

From early 2008 local authorities, through community planning processes, assumed autonomy for how they choose to deliver local services. The provision of services to young offenders is now delivered within the context of the Concordat between central and local government. Yet the focus on service provision as the vehicle for delivery of outcomes has implications not only for effective multi-agency working but the impact on the young person. Of the 15 national outcomes included in the Concordat, a number have direct relevance to the youth offending agenda, including the management of children and young people who present a risk of serious harm. The national outcomes include ensuring that young people are successful learners, confident individuals, effective contributors and responsible citizens; that the life chances for children, young people and families at risk are improved; that we live our lives safe from crime, disorder and danger; that we have strong, resilient and supportive communities where people take responsibility for their own actions and how they affect others; that our public services are high quality, continually improving, efficient and responsive to local people's needs.

Restorative justice

In this book we have considered alternative approaches and have argued that the ethos of restorative justice, for example, fits well within the current youth justice system in Scotland. It provides a somewhat different approach from either the welfare or punitive models and focuses our attention on the victims of crime or those who have been harmed. Yet the future for restorative youth justice in Scotland remains unclear. The Scottish Government has yet to embrace fully restorative justice, although there is support for its underlying principles, the effects of which can be seen in many different guises in Scottish responses to youth offending. One difficulty facing the Scottish Government is the provision of a clear and workable definition in order to inform and allow evaluations of the effectiveness of these processes. Robust evaluation is required in order to move away from the portrayal (and perception) of restorative justice practice as a 'soft option'. The recent government publication *Restorative Justice Services for Children and Young People and Those They Have Harmed* (2008j) provides national guidelines for those offering restorative justice services, recognising that more needs to be done to ensure clear understanding of what restorative justice is. To this end a National Evaluation Project was started in 2008 in order to assess the different practices and their adherence to the national guidance published in 2007 (*Best Practice Guidance for Restorative Justice Practitioners and their Case Supervisors and Line Managers (Scotland)*). Public awareness of how restorative practice works is important, not only in terms of procedure but also for the outcomes for victims, offenders and the community.

Public awareness, public confidence

In the years leading up to devolution and since then, matters of crime and criminal justice have become a staple of the Scottish political agenda, and youth crime and youth justice in particular have become increasingly politicised. At the same time, the 'problem of youth crime' has been afforded intense attention from the Scottish media. Stories routinely juxtapose youth crime and the public's 'right to safety', disputing whether justice is done and encouraging less tolerant societal attitudes towards young people's behaviour. There is a clear disjuncture between, on the one hand, media-driven perceptions that youth crime is a major social problem and that many local communities are terrorised by violent youth gangs and adversely affected by anti-social behaviour and, on the other hand, the stark, if more mundane, reality of youth crime, as measured by crime surveys, official statistics etc., and derived from robust research evidence. The depiction of communities under siege by rampant bands of miscreant and disaffected youth is routinely found in many other western jurisdictions, and is certainly not solely a Scottish problem. Yet there is little doubt that Scotland's public do need to be better informed about the nature and extent of youth crime and the operation and delivery of youth justice. There is considerable scope and opportunity to address the matter of public awareness in the context of the current governmental aim of increasing and maintaining confidence in the justice system. It should not be too much to hope for.

Note

1 The Children's Hearings (Scotland) Bill was published in June 2009 and is available from URL: www.scotland.gov.uk/Publications/2009/06/29113351/2

References and Further Reading

Anderson, S., Kinsey, R., Loader, I. and Grove, C. (1994). *Cautionary Tales: Young People, Policing and Crime in Edinburgh*, Aldershot: Avebury

Anderson, S., Bromley, C and Given, L. (2005) *Public Attitudes Towards Young People and Youth Crime in Scotland: Findings from the 2004 Social Attitudes Study*, Edinburgh: Scottish Executive. Available from URL: www.scotland.gov.uk/Publications/2005/07/1485403/54066

Asquith, S. (1983) *Children and Justice: Decision-making in Children's Hearings and Juvenile Courts*, Edinburgh: Edinburgh University Press

Asquith, S. (1996) 'When children kill children: the search for justice', *Childhood*, Vol. 3, No. 1, pp. 99–116

Asquith, S. and Docherty, M. (1999) 'Preventing offending by children and young people in Scotland', in P. Duff and N. Hutton (eds) (1999) *Criminal Justice in Scotland*, Aldershot: Dartmouth

Asquith, S. and Hill, M. (eds.) (1991) *Justice for Children*, Dordrecht: Martinus Nijhoff

Asquith, S. and Samuel, E. (1994) *Criminal Justice and Related Services for Young Adult Offenders: A Review*, Edinburgh: HMSO

Atkinson, R. and Helms, G. (eds) (2007) *Securing an Urban Renaissance: Crime, Community and British Urban Policy*, Bristol: Policy Press

Audit Scotland (2001) *Youth Justice in Scotland: A Baseline Report*, Edinburgh: Audit Scotland

Audit Scotland (2002) *Dealing with Offending by Young People: Main Report*, Edinburgh: Audit Scotland

Audit Scotland (2007) *Dealing with Offending by Young People: Performance Update*, Edinburgh, Audit Scotland

Ball, C. (2004) 'Youth justice: half a century of response to youth offending', *Criminal Law Review* (Mar), 167–80

Batchelor, S. and Burman, M. (2004) 'Working with girls and young women', in McIvor, G. (ed.) (2004) *Women Who Offend*, Research Highlights in Social Work 44, London: Jessica Kingsley

Blunkett, D. (2001) *Politics and Progress:Renewing Democracy and Civil Society*, London: Politicos

Bottoms, A. and Dignan, J. (2004) 'Youth justice in Great Britain', *Crime and Justice*, Vol. 31

Bradshaw, P. (2005) *On the Right Track*, Stirling: SCRA

Brown, M. and Bolling, K. (2007) *2006 Scottish Crime and Victimisation Survey: Main Findings*, Edinburgh: Scottish Government

Bruce, N. and Spencer, J. (1976) *Face to Face with Families: A Report on the Children's Panels in Scotland*, Loanhead: Macdonald

Bryce, D. (2005) *Alive and Kicking: A Story of Crime, Addiction and Redemption in Glasgow's Gangland*, Edinburgh: Mainstream Publishing

Buist, M. and Whyte, B. (2004) 'Decision Making and Services Relating to Children and Young People Involved in Offending' (online). Available from URL: www.scotland.gov. uk/Resource/Doc/26800/0023678.pdf

Burman, M., Bradshaw, P., Hutton, N., McNeill, F. and Munro, M. (2006) 'The end of an era? Youth justice in Scotland', in Junger-Tas, J. and Decker, S. (eds) International Handbook of Juvenile Justice, Dordrecht: Springer

Burman, M., Armstrong, S., Batchelor, S. and McNeill, F. (2007) *Risk Assessment and Risk Management of Children and Young People Engaging in Offending Behaviour*, Paisley: Risk Management Authority

Burman, M., Johnstone, J., Fraser, A. and McNeill, F. (2009) 'Scotland', in Dünkel, F., Grzywa, J., Horsfield, P. and Pruin, I. (eds) (2009) *Juvenile Justice Systems in Europe – current situation, reform developments and good practices*, Mönchengladbach: Forum Verlag Godesberg

Burney, E. (2005) *Making People Behave: Anti-social Behaviour, Politics and Policy*, Cullompton: Willan

Campbell, B. (1993) *Goliath: Britain's Dangerous Places*, London: Methuen

Cavanagh, B. (2007) *A Review of Dispersal Powers*, Edinburgh: Scottish Government

Children's Hearings, www.childrens-hearings.co.uk

Coleman, C. and Moynihan, J. (1996) *Understanding Crime Data: Haunted by the Dark Figure*, Buckingham: Open University Press

Commission of the European Communities (2001), *European Commission White Paper: A New Impetus for European Youth*, COM (2001) 681, Brussels: European Commission. Available from URL: http://ec.europa.eu/youth/archive/whitepaper/download/ whitepaper_en.pdf (accessed 9 September 2009)

Council Framework Decision 2001 on the Standing of Victims in the Criminal Justice System, OJEU L 82 of 22.3.2001, p. 1

Crawford, A. (1998) *Crime Prevention and Community Safety*, London: Longman

Crawford, A. and Newburn, T. (2003) *Youth Offending and Restorative Justice*, Cullompton: Willan

Croall, H. (2006) 'Criminal justice in post devolutionary Scotland', *Critical Social Policy*, Vol. 26, No. 3, 587–607

Curran, J., MacQueen, S., Whyte, B. with Boyle, J. (2007) *Forced to Make Amends: An Evaluation of the Community Reparation Order Pilots*, Edinburgh: CJSW Development Centre, University of Edinburgh

Davies, N. (1998) *Dark Heart: The Shocking Truth about Hidden Britain*. London: Vintage

Dewar, S. and Payne, J. (2003) *Anti-Social Behaviour: An Overview*, Edinburgh: Scottish Parliament: SPICe Briefing 03/70

Dewar, S. (2003) *Anti-Social Behaviour: Key Issues and Debates*, Edinburgh: The Scottish Parliament: SPICe Briefing 03/72

DTZ and Heriot Watt University (2007) *Use of Antisocial Behaviour Orders in Scotland: report of the 2005/06 survey*, Edinburgh: Scottish Executive

DTZ Consulting and Research (2007) *An Evaluation of Local Authority Antisocial Neighbour Noise Nuisance Services*, Edinburgh: Scottish Government. Available from URL: www.scotland.gov.uk/Publications/2007/10/24132337/4

DTZ Pieda Consulting (2005) *Measurement of the extent of youth crime in Scotland*, Edinburgh: Scottish Executive. Available from URL: www.scotland.gov.uk/ Publications/2005/03/31141334/13490

Duquette, D. (1994) 'Scottish Children's Hearings and representation for the child', in Asquith, S. and Hill, M. (eds) (1994) *Justice for Children,* Netherlands: Martinus Nijhoff

Eberst, A. and Staines, H. (2006) *Evaluation of the 12-month Fixed Penalty Notice Pilot in the Tayside Police Force Area,* Dundee: University of Abertay Dundee/Tayside Police

Ewing Review (2007) *Community Safety and Antisocial Behaviour Policy Update,* Edinburgh: Scottish Government

Ewing Review (2008) *Review of the National Antisocial Behaviour Strategy –1st Progress Report,* Edinburgh: Scottish Government

Farrington, D. (1996) *Understanding and Preventing Youth Crime,* York: Joseph Rowntree Foundation

Finlayson, A. (1976) 'The Reporter', in Martin, F. M. and Murray, M. (eds) (1991) *Children's Hearings,* Edinburgh: Scottish Academic Press

Finlayson, A. (1992) *Reporters to Children's Panels: Their Role, Function and Accountability,* Edinburgh: HMSO

Fionda, J. (2005) *Devils and Angels: Youth, Policy and Crime,* Oxford: Hart

Flint, J. (ed.) (2006) *Housing, Urban Governance and Anti-social Behaviour: Perspectives, Policy and Practice,* Bristol: Policy Press

Flint, J., Atkinson, R. and Scott, S. (2003) *Report on the Consultation Responses to Putting our Communities First: A Strategy for Tackling Anti-social Behaviour,* Edinburgh: Scottish Executive

Flint, J. *et al.* (2007) *The Impact of Local Antisocial Behaviour Strategies at the Neighbourhood Level. Research Findings 6.2007,* Edinburgh: Scottish Government. Available from URL: www.scotland.gov.uk/Publications/2007/10/18103649/0

Flood-Page, C., Campbell, S., Harrington, V. and Miller, J. (2000) *Youth Crime, Findings from the 1998/99 Youth Lifestyles Survey,* Home Office Research Study 209, Home Office: London

Fox, S. (1991) *Children's Hearings and the International Community: The Kilbrandon Child Care Lecture,* Edinburgh: HMSO

Furlong, A. and Cartmel, F. (1997) *Young People and Social Change,* Buckingham: Open University Press

Garland, D. (2001) *The Culture of Control: Crime and Social Order in Contemporary Society,* Oxford: Oxford University Press

Gelsthorpe, L. and Morris, A. (1994) 'Juvenile justice 1945–1992', in Maguire, M., Morgan, R. and Reiner, R. (eds) (1994) *The Oxford Handbook of Criminology,* Oxford: Clarendon

Genn, H. (1993) 'Alternative dispute resolution and civil justice: an unresolved dispute', *The Modern Law Review,* Vol. 56, No. 3, pp. 393–411

Graham, J. and Bowling, B. (1995) *Young People and Crime,* Home Office Research Study No. 145, London, HMSO

Griffiths, A. and Kandel, R. (2006) 'Children's confidentiality at the crossroad: challenges for the Scottish Children's Hearings System', *Journal of Social Welfare and Family Law,* Vol. 28, No. 2, pp. 137–52

Hagell, A. and Newburn, T. (1994) *Persistent Young Offenders,* London: Policy Studies Institute

Hallett, C. and Hazel, N. (1998) *The Evaluation of Children's Hearings in Scotland, Volume 2, The International Context: Trends in Juvenile Justice and Child Welfare,* Edinburgh: Scottish Office Central Research Unit

Hallett, C. and Murray, C. with Jamieson, J. and Veitch, B. (1998) *The Evaluation of Children's Hearings in Scotland, Volume 1: Deciding in Children's Interests*, Edinburgh: Scottish Office Central Research Unit

Hanley, L. (2007) *Estates: An Intimate History*, London: Granta

Hayton, K., Boyd, C., Campbell, M., Crawford, K., Latimer, K., Lindsay, S. And Percy, V. (2007) *Evaluation of the Impact and Implementation of Community Wardens*, Edinburgh: Scottish Government. Available from URL: www.scotland.gov.uk/ Publications/2007/03/22104147/0

Hill, M., Walker, M., Moodie, K., Wallace, B., Bannister, J., Khan, F., McIvor, G. and Kendrick, A. (2005) *Fast Track Children's Hearings Pilot*, Edinburgh: Scottish Executive Social Research

Hill, M., Walker, M., Moodie K., Wallace B., Bannister, J., Khan, F., McIvor, G. and Kendrick, A. (2007a) 'More haste, less speed? An evaluation of fast track policies to tackle persistent youth offending in Scotland', *Youth Justice*, Vol. 7, No. 2, 121–38

Hill, M., Lockyer, A. and Stone, F. (2007b) *Youth Justice and Child Protection*, London: Jessica Kingsley

Hindelang, M. J., Hirschi, T. and Weis, J. G. (1981) *Measuring Delinquency*, Beverley Hills, CA: Sage

Holman, B. (1997) *FARE Dealing: Neighbourhood Involvement in a Housing Scheme*, London: Community Development Foundation

Home Office (2003) *Respect and Responsibility: Taking a Stand Against Anti-social Behaviour*, Cm 5778. Available from URL: www.archive2.official-documents.co.uk/ document/cm57/5778/5778.pdf

Howard League for Penal Reform (2007) Children as Victims: Child-sized Crimes in a Child-sized World, London: The Howard League

Hughes, G. (1998) *Understanding Crime Prevention*, Buckingham: Open University Press.

Hughes, G. and Edwards, A. (2005) 'Crime prevention in context', in Tilley, N. (ed.) (2005) *Handbook of Crime Prevention and Community Safety*, Devon: Willan Publishing

Huizinga, D. And Elliott, D. S. (1986) 'Reassessing the reliability and validity of self-report delinquency measures, *Journal of Quantitative Criminology*, Vol. 2, No. 4, pp. 293–327

Jamieson, J., McIvor, G. And Murray, C. (1999) *Understanding offending among young people*, Edinburgh: Scottish Executive

Junger-Tas, J. (1994) 'The International Self-Report Delinquency Study: some methodological and theoretical issues', in Junger-Tas, J., Terlouw, G. J. and Klein, M. W. (eds) *Delinquent Behaviour among Young People in the Western World*, Amsterdam: Kugler Publications

Karp, D. And Clear, T. (eds) (2002) *What is Community Justice? Case Studies of Restorative Justice and Community Supervision*, London: Sage

Kearney, B. (1998) 'The relationships between courts and hearings', in Lockyer, A. and Stone, F. H. (eds) (1998) *Juvenile Justice in Scotland: 25 Years of the Welfare Approach*. Edinburgh: T&T Clark

Kearney, B. (2000) *Children's Hearings and the Sheriff Court* (2nd edition), Edinburgh: Butterworth

Kelly, A. (1996) *Introduction to the Scottish Children's Panel*, Winchester: Waterside Press

Kilbrandon Report (1964) *Children and Young Persons (Scotland)*, Cmnd 2306, Edinburgh: HMSO

Liddle, M. and Solanki, A. (2002) *Persistent Young Offenders*, London: Nacro

Lockyer, A. (1992) *Citizen's Service and Children's Panel Membership*, Edinburgh: The Scottish Office

Lockyer, A. and Stone, F. H. (eds) (1998a) *Juvenile Justice in Scotland: 25 Years of the Welfare Approach*, Edinburgh: T&T Clark

Lockyer, A. and Stone, F.H. (1998b) 'The Kilbrandon origins', in Lockyer, A. and Stone, F. H. (eds) (1998) *Juvenile Justice in Scotland: 25 Years of the Welfare Approach*, Edinburgh: T&T Clark

Macdivitt, K. (2008) *Evaluation of the Structured Deferred Sentence Pilots*, Edinburgh: Scottish Government

Marshall, T. (1999) *Restorative justice: an overview*, London: Home Office

Martin, F. M. (1978) 'The future of juvenile justice: English courts and Scottish Hearings', *Howard Journal of Penology and Crime Prevention*, Vol. 17, No. 2, pp. 78–89

Martin, F. M. and Murray, K. (eds) (1976) *Children's Hearings*, Edinburgh: Scottish Academic Press

Martin, F. M. and Murray, K. (eds) (1982) *The Scottish Juvenile Justice System*, Edinburgh: Scottish Academic Press

Martin, F. M., Fox, S. and Murray, M. (1981) *Children Out of Court*, Edinburgh: Scottish Academic Press

McAra, L. (1998) *Social Work and Criminal Justice. Volume 2: Early Arrangements*, Edinburgh: The Stationery Office

McAra, L. (2002) 'The Scottish juvenile justice system: policy and practice', in Winterdyk, J. (ed.) (2002) *Juvenile Justice Systems: International perspectives* (2nd edition), Toronto: Canadian Scholars Press

McAra, L. (2004) 'The cultural and institutional dynamics of transformation: youth justice in Scotland and England and Wales', *Cambrian Law Review*, Vol. 35, pp. 23–54

McAra, L. (2006) 'Welfare in crisis? Key developments in Scottish youth justice', in Muncie, J. and Goldson, B. (eds) (2006) *Comparative Youth Justice: Critical Issues*, London: Sage

McAra, L. (2008) 'Crime, criminology and criminal justice in Scotland', in *European Journal of Criminology*, Vol. 5, No. 4, pp. 481–504

McAra, L. and McVie, S. (2005) 'The usual suspects? Street-life, young offenders and the police', *Criminal Justice,* Vol. 5, No. 1, pp. 5–35

McAra, L. and McVie, S. (2007) 'Youth justice? The impact of system contact on patterns of desistance from offending', *European Journal of Criminology,* Vol. 4, No. 3, pp. 315–45

McGhee, J. and Waterhouse, L. (2002) 'Family support and the Scottish children's Hearings system', *Child and Family Social Work,* Vol. 7, No. 4, pp. 273–83

McDiarmid, C. (2005) 'Welfare, offending and the Scottish Children's Hearing System', *Journal of Social Welfare and Family Law*, Vol. 27, No. 1, pp. 31–42

McIvor, G. (2004) (ed.) *Women Who Offend*, Research Highlights in Social Work 44, London: Jessica Kingsley

McIvor, G. and McNeill, F. (2007) 'Developments in probation in Scotland' in McIvor, G. and Raynor, P. (eds), *Developments in Social Work with Offenders: Research Highlights in Social Work 48*, London: Jessica Kingsley

McIvor, G., Malloch, M., Brown, A., Murray, C., Eley, S., Piacentini, L. and Walters, R. (2004) *The Hamilton Sheriff Youth Court Pilot: The First Six Months*, Edinburgh:

Scottish Executive Social Research

McIvor, G., Barnsdale, L., MacRae, R., Dunlop, S., Brown, A., Eley, S., Malloch, M., Murray, C., Murray, L., Piacentini, L., Popham, F. and Walters, R. (2006) *Evaluation of the Airdrie and Hamilton Youth Court Pilots*, Edinburgh: Scottish Executive Social Research. Available from URL: www.scotland.gov.uk/Publications/2006/06/13155406/0

McNeill, F. (2006) 'Community supervision: context and relationships matter', in Goldson, B. and Muncie, J. (eds) (2006) *Youth Crime and Justice*, London: Sage

McNeill, F. and Batchelor, S. (2002) 'Chaos, containment and change: responding to persistent offending by young people', *Youth Justice*, Vol. 2, No. 1, pp. 27–43

McNeill, F. and Batchelor, S. (2004) *Persistent Offending by Young People: Developing Practice. Issues in Community and Criminal Justice Monograph No. 4*, London: National Association of Probation Officers

McNeill, F., Batchelor, S., Burnett, R. and Knox J. (2005) *21st Century Social Work. Reducing Re-offending: Key Practice Skills*, Edinburgh: Scottish Executive

Mooney, J. and Young, J. (2006) 'The decline in crime and the rise of anti-social behaviour', *Probation Journal*, Vol. 53, No. 4, pp. 397– 407

Moore, G. and Whyte, B. (1998) *Social Work and Criminal Law in Scotland*, Edinburgh: Mercat Press

MORI (2001) *Youth Survey 2001 for the Youth Justice Board for England and Wales*, London: YJB

MORI Scotland (2003) *The Glasgow Youth Survey 2003*. Available from URL: www. glasgow.gov.uk/NR/rdonlyres/36479108-9262-4E7C-82B8-B2F3022387EA/0/youthsurvey.pdf (accessed 9 September 2009)

Morris, A. and Giller, H. (1987) *Understanding Juvenile Justice*, Kent: Croom Helm

Morris, A. and McIsaac, M. (1978) *Juvenile Justice? A Case Study of the Operation of Children's Hearings in Scotland*, Heinemann: London

Muncie, J. (1999) *Youth and Crime: A Critical Introduction*, London: Sage

Muncie, J. (2004) *Youth and Crime: A Critical Introduction* (2nd edition), London: Sage

Muncie, J. and Goldson, B. (2006) (eds) *Comparative Youth Justice: Critical Issues* London: Sage

Muncie, J., Hughes, G. and McLaughlin, E. (eds) (2002) *Youth Justice: Critical Readings*, London: Sage

Murray, C., Hallett, C., McMillan, N. and Watson, J. (2002) *Home Supervision. Scotland's Children, Children (Scotland) Act 1995 (Research Findings No. 4)*, Edinburgh: Scottish Executive

NACRO (2001) *Some Facts about Young People who Offend*, London, Nacro

NCH Scotland (2003) *Where's Kilbrandon Now? Report and Recommendations from the Inquiry*, NCH Scotland

Nellis, M. (2000) 'Creating community justice', in Pease, K., McLaren, V. and Ballantyne, S. (eds) (2000) *Secure Foundations: Key Issues in Crime Prevention, Reduction and Community Safety*, London: IPPR

Newburn, T. (2002a) 'The Contemporary Politics of Youth Crime Prevention', in Muncie, J., Hughes, G. and McLaughlin, E. (eds) (2002) *Youth Justice: Critical Readings*, London: Sage

Newburn, T. (2002b) 'Young people, crime and youth justice', in Maguire, M., Morgan, R. and Reiner, R. (eds) (2002) *The Oxford Handbook of Criminology* (3rd edition), Oxford University Press: Oxford

Newburn, T. (ed.) (2007a) *Criminology*, Devon: Willan Publishing

Newburn, T. (2007b) 'Youth crime and youth culture', in Maguire, M., Morgan, R. and Reiner, R. (eds) (2007) *The Oxford Handbook of Criminology* (4th edition), Oxford: Oxford University Press

Nichols, G. (2007) *Sport and Crime Reduction: The Role of Sports in Tackling Youth Crime*, London: Routledge

Norrie, K. (1995) *The Children Scotland Act 1995*, Reading: W. Green

Norrie, K. (1997) *Children's Hearings in Scotland*, Edinburgh: W. Green/Sweet and Maxwell

Ollenburger, J. C. (1986) 'Panel members' attitudes towards justice', *British Journal of Criminology*, Vol. 26, No. 4, pp. 372–84

PA Consulting Group (2004) *Scottish Youth Justice Baseline*, PA: Glasgow

Packer, H. (1968) *The Limits of the Criminal Sanction*, Stanford: Stanford University Press

Paton, L. (2004) 'Children's Hearings in Scotland: 40 years after Kilbrandon', *Childright*, No. 205, pp. 7–9

Pawson, H. and McKenzie, C. (2006) 'Social landlords, anti-social behaviour and countermeasures', in Flint, J. (ed.) (2006) *Housing, Urban Governance and Anti-Social Behaviour: Perspectives, Policy and Practice*, Bristol: Policy Press

Payne, J. (2003) *Anti-Social Behaviour: Putting our Communities First*, Edinburgh: Scottish Parliament: SPICe Briefing 03/71

Petch, A. (1988) 'Answering back: parental perspectives on the children's hearings system', *British Journal of Social Work*, Vol. 18, No.1, pp. 1–24

Piacentini, L. and Walters, R. (2006) 'The politicization of youth crime in Scotland and the rise of the "Burberry Court"', *Youth Justice*, Vol. 6, No. 1, pp. 43–59

Popham, F., McIvor, G., Brown, A., Eley, S., Malloch, M., Murray, C., Piacentini, L. and Walters, R. (2005) *Evaluation of the Hamilton Sheriff Youth Court Pilot 2003–2005*, Edinburgh: Scottish Executive

Prior, D. (2007) *Continuities and Discontinuities in Governing Anti-Social Behaviour*, Birmingham: University of Birmingham, Institute of Applied Social Studies

Restorative Justice Consortium (2004), *Principles of Restorative Processes*. London: Restorative Justice Consortium. Available from URL: www.restorativejustice.org. uk/?Resources:Best_Practice:Principles

Retzinger, S. M. and Scheff, T. J. (1996) 'Strategy for community conferences', in Galaway, B. and Hudson, J. (eds) (1996) *Restorative Justice: International Perspectives*, Monsey, NY: Criminal Justice Press

Ruiz, J. (2004) *Education Dept Research Findings No 2: A Literature Review of the Evidence Base for Culture, the Arts and Sport Policy*, Edinburgh: Scottish Executive. Available from URL: www.scotland.gov.uk/Resource/Doc/17002/0029574.pdf

S v. *Miller* 2001 SC 977

Scott, S. (2006) 'Tackling antisocial behaviour: an evaluation of the Dundee Families Project', in Flint, J. (ed.) (2006) *Housing, Urban Governance and Anti-social Behaviour: Perspectives, Policy and Practice*, Bristol: Policy Press

Scottish Children's Reporter Administration (SCRA), www.scra.gov.uk

Scottish Children's Reporter Administration (2006) *Scottish Children's Reporter Administration Annual Report 2005/2006*, Stirling: SCRA. Available from URL: www.scra.gov. uk/cms_resources/Annual%20Report%202005-2006.pdf

Scottish Children's Reporter Administration (2007) *Persistent Young Offenders. A Study of Children Identified as Persistent Young Offenders in Scotland*, Stirling: SCRA

Scottish Council on Tribunals (2002) 'Special Report: Children's Hearings System' (online). Available from URL: www.council-on-tribunals.gov.uk/scottish/394.htm

Scottish Education Department/Scottish Home and Health Department (1966) *Social work in the Community*, Cmnd 3065, Edinburgh: HMSO

Scottish Executive (1996) *Criminal Proceedings in Scottish Courts, 1996*. Available from URL: http://search1.scotland.gov.uk/Scotland?n=All&rcexpanded=false&action=search&q=Criminal+Proceedings+in+Scottish+Courts

Scottish Executive (1997) *Review of Youth Crime: Preventing and Responding to Criminal Behaviour by Children and Young People: a Summary Paper*, Edinburgh: Scottish Executive. Available from URL: www.scotland.gov.uk/youth/crimereview/summary.asp

Scottish Executive (2000a) *It's a Criminal Waste: Stop Youth Crime Now: The Report of the Advisory Group on Youth Crime*, Edinburgh: Scottish Executive. Available from URL: www.scotland.gov.uk/youth/crimereview/

Scottish Executive (2000b) *The Scottish Executive's Response to the Advisory Group Report on Youth Crime*, The Scottish Executive: Edinburgh

Scottish Executive (2002a) *National Standards for Scotland's Youth Justice Services: A Report by the Improving the Effectiveness of the Youth Justice System Working Group*, Edinburgh: Scottish Executive

Scottish Executive (2002b) *Scotland's Action Programme to Reduce Youth Crime*, Edinburgh: Scottish Executive

Scottish Executive (2002c) *The Ten Point Action Plan for Tackling Youth Crime* Edinburgh: Scottish Executive

Scottish Executive (2003a) *A Partnership for a Better Scotland*, Edinburgh: Scottish Executive

Scottish Executive (2003b) *Putting Our Communities First: A Strategy for Tackling Antisocial Behaviour*, Edinburgh: Scottish Executive

Scottish Executive (2004a) *Getting it Right for Every Child: Consultation Pack on the Review of the Children's Hearing System*, Edinburgh: Scottish Executive

Scottish Executive (2004b) *Guidelines on a New National System of Police Warnings for Children and Young Offenders with a Restorative Element*, Edinburgh: Scottish Executive. Available from URL: www.scotland.gov.uk/Publications/2004/06/19497/38775

Scottish Executive (2005) 'Restorative justice services in the Children's Hearing System' (online). Available from URL: www.scotland.gov.uk/Publications/2005/07/11160004/00062

Scottish Executive (2006a) *Criminal Justice Social Work Statistics, 2005*, Edinburgh: Scottish Executive

Scottish Executive (2006 newb) *National Standards for Community Engagement*: Edinburgh: Scottish Executive

Scottish Executive (2006b newc) *Recorded Crime in Scotland, 2005/06* Statistical Bulletin CrJ 2006/6, Criminal Justice Series, Edinburgh: Scottish Executive

Scottish Executive (2006c newd) *Secure Accommodation in Scotland: Its Role and Relationship with 'Alternative Services'*, Edinburgh: Scottish Executive

Scottish Executive (2006d newe) Statistical Bulletin: CrJ/2006/01: Prison Statistics Scotland, 2005/06 Edinburgh: Scottish Executive. Available from URL: www.scotland.gov.uk/Resource/Doc/91611/0021855.pdf

Scottish Executive (2006e newf) *Statistical Bulletin: CrJ/2006/5: Prison Statistics Scotland, 2005/06*, Edinburgh: Scottish Executive. Available from URL: www.scotland.gov.uk/

Publications/2006/08/18103613/3

Scottish Executive (2006f newg, June update) *Ten point action plan on youth crime*, Edinburgh: Scottish Executive

Scottish Executive (2006g newh) *Youth Justice Improvement Programme*, Edinburgh: Scottish Executive

Scottish Executive (2006h newi) *Youth Justice National Standards: Progress to March 2006 Summary Report*. Available from URL: www.scotland.gov.uk/Publications/2006/07/11085731/1

Scottish Executive (2007) *Statistical Bulletin Prison Statistics: CrJ 2007/7, Scotland 2006/07*, Edinburgh: Scottish Government. Available from URL: www.scotland.gov.uk/Resource/Doc/196743/0052707.pdf

Scottish Executive Education Department (2004) *Children's Panel Members Survey 2004: Children's Panel Members' Views on CPAC*, Edinburgh: Scottish Executive (online). Available from URL: www.childrens-hearings.co.uk/pdf/CPAC%20Seminar%202004.pdf

Scottish Executive Education Department (2006) *Insight 33: Report on Secure Accommodation in Scotland*, Edinburgh: Scottish Executive

Scottish Executive Education Department (2007) *Scotland's Children's Panels: Annual Report 2006*, Edinburgh: Scottish Executive (online). Available from URL: www.childrens-hearings.co.uk/doc/2007/03/REQ20072131149694.doc

Scottish Government (2007a) *Criminal Proceedings in Scottish Courts 2005/06*, Statistical Bulletin Crime and Justice Series, Edinburgh: Scottish Government

Scottish Government (2007b) *Recorded Crime in Scotland, 2006/07*, Statistical Bulletin CrJ, Criminal Justice Series, Edinburgh: Scottish Government

Scottish Government (2008a) *Abolition of Unruly Certificates Section 51(1)(bb) and 51(3) Criminal Procedure (Scotland) Act 1995, Scottish Government Joint Consultation by Care and Justice Division and Criminal Procedure Division on alternative proposals*, Edinburgh: Scottish Government

Scottish Government (2008b) *Criminal Proceedings in Scottish Courts 2006/07*, Statistical Bulletin Crime and Justice Series, Edinburgh: Scottish Government

Scottish Government (2008c) *Evaluation of Intensive Support and Monitoring Services (ISMS) within the Children's Hearings System*, Scottish Government: Edinburgh

Scottish Government (2008d) *Evaluation of the Implementation of and Impact of the Glasgow Anti-Social Behaviour Taskforce*, Edinburgh: Scottish Government

Scottish Government (2008e) *Getting It Right for Children and Young People who Present a Risk of Serious Harm*, Edinburgh: Scottish Government

Scottish Government (2008 newf) *HM Chief Inspector of Prisons for Scotland: Annual Report 2007-2008, SE 2008/162*, Edinburgh: Scottish Government

Scottish Government (2008f newg) *Preventing Offending by Young People: A Framework for Action*, Edinburgh: Scottish Government

Scottish Government (2008g newh) *Protecting Scotland's Communities: Fair Fast and Flexible Justice*, Edinburgh: Scottish Government

Scottish Government (2008h newi) *Recorded Crime in Scotland, 2006/07*, Statistical Bulletin Crime and Justice Series, Edinburgh: Scottish Government

Scottish Government (2008i newj) *Restorative Justice Services for Children and Young People and Those Harmed by their Behaviour*, Edinburgh: Scottish Government. Available from URL: www.scotland.gov.uk/Publications/2008/06/10143757/0

Scottish Government (2008j newk) *Strengthening for the Future: A Consultation on the Reform of the Children's Hearings System*, Edinburgh: Scottish Government

Scottish Government (2009a) *Criminal Proceedings in Scottish Courts, 2007/08*, Statistical Bulletin, Edinburgh: Scottish Government

Scottish Government (2009b) *Promoting Positive Outcomes: Working Together to Prevent Antisocial Behaviour in Scotland – Volume 1 (The Ewing Report)*, Edinburgh: Scottish Government. Available from URL: www.scotland.gov.uk/Resource/Doc/264302/0079222.pdf (accessed 9 September 2009)

Scottish Government (2009c) *Securing our Future Initiative: A Way Forward for Scotland's Secure Care Estate. A response from the Scottish Government and COSLA*, Edinburgh: Scottish Government

Scottish Home and Health Department/Scottish Education Department (1964/1995) *Children and Young Persons, Scotland*, Cmnd 2306, (Kilbrandon Report), Edinburgh: HMSO. Available from URL: www.scotland.gov.uk/Publications/2003/10/18259/26900

Scottish Law Commission (2002), *Report on the Age of Criminal Responsibility*, SE/2002/1, Edinburgh: Scottish Executive

Scottish Office (1993) *Scotland's Children: Proposals for Child Care Policy and Law*, Cmnd 2286, Edinburgh: HMSO

Scottish Office (1996) *'A Secure Remedy': A Review of Secure Care in Scotland*, Scottish Office: Edinburgh

Scottish Parliament (2009) Criminal Justice and Licensing (Scotland) Bill (SP Bill 24). Available from URL: www.scottish.parliament.uk/s3/bills/24-CrimJustLc/index.htm

Scottish Prisons Commission (2008) *Scotland's Choice – report of the Scottish Prisons Commission*, Edinburgh: Scottish Prisons Commission. Available from URL: www.scotland.gov.uk/Resource/Doc/230180/0062359.pdf

Seed, P. and Lloyd, M. G. (1997) *Quality of Life*, London: Jessica Kingsley

Shapland, J., Atkinson, A., Colledge, E., Dignan, J., Howes, M., Johnstone, J., Pennant, R., Robinson, G. and Sorsby, A. (2004) *Implementing Restorative Justice Schemes (Crime Reduction Programme): A Report on the First Year*, Home Office Online Report 32/04, London: Home Office. Available from URL: www.homeoffice.gov.uk/rds/pdfs04/rdsolr3204.pdf.

Shapland, J., Atkinson, A., Atkinson, H., Chapman, B., Colledge, E., Dignan, J., Howes, M., Johnstone, J., Robinson, G. and Sorsby, A. (2006a), *Restorative Justice in Practice: The Second Report from the Evaluation of Three Schemes*, The University of Sheffield Centre for Criminological Research. Available from URL: www.shef.ac.uk/content/1/c6/07/76/55/Restorative%20Justice%20Report%20-%20final%20version.pdf

Shapland, J., Atkinson, A., Atkinson, H., Colledge, E., Dignan, J., Howes, M., Johnstone J., Robinson, G. and Sorsby, A. (2006b) 'Situating restorative justice within criminal justice', *Theoretical Criminology*, Vol. 10, No. 4, pp. 505–32

Shapland, J., Atkinson, A., Atkinson, H., Chapman, B., Dignan, J., Howes, M., Johnstone, J., Robinson, G. and Sorsby, A. (2007) *Restorative Justice: The Views of Victims and Offenders*, Ministry of Justice Research Series 3/07, London: Ministry of Justice. Available from URL: www.justice.gov.uk/docs/Restorative-Justice.pdf

Shapland, J., Atkinson, A., Atkinson, H., Dignan, J., Edwards, L., Hibbert, J., Howes, M., Johnstone, J., Robinson, G. and Sorsby, A. (2008) *Does Restorative Justice Affect Reconviction? The Fourth Report from the Evaluation of Three Schemes*, London: Ministry of Justice

Shaw, J. (1966) 'Children in trouble', *British Journal of Criminology*, Vol. 6, No. 2, pp. 112–22

Simon, J. (2007) *Governing through Crime: How the War on Crime Transformed American*

Democracy and Created a Culture of Fear, New York: Oxford University Press

Smith, D. J. and McAra, L. (2004) *Gender and Youth Offending*, Edinburgh Study of Youth Transitions and Crime Research Digest No. 2.

Smith, D. and McVie, S. (2003) 'Theory and method in the Edinburgh study of youth transitions and crime', *British Journal of Criminology*, Vol. 43, pp. 169–95

Smith, D. and Young, P. (1999) 'Crime trends in Scotland since 1950', in Duff, P. and Hutton, N. (eds) (1999) *Criminal Justice in Scotland*, Dartmouth: Ashgate

Soothill, K., Francis, B., Ackerley, E. and Humphreys, L. (2008) 'Changing patterns of offending behaviour among young adults', *British Journal of Criminology*, Vol. 48, No. 1, pp. 75–95

Squires, P. (ed.) (2008) *ASBO Nation: The Criminalisation of Nuisance*, Bristol: Polity Press

Stone, F. (1995) 'Introduction', *The Kilbrandon Report: Children and Young Persons, Scotland*, Edinburgh: HMSO

Thomson, J. M. (1991) *Family Law in Scotland* (2nd edition), Edinburgh: Butterworth

Tisdall, K.(1997) *The Children (Scotland) Act 1995: Developing Policy and Law for Scotland's Children*, Edinburgh: The Stationery Office

Tonry, M. and Doob, A. (eds) (2004) *Youth Crime and Youth Justice: Comparative and Cross-national perspectives. A Review of Research, Crime and Justice*, Vol 31, Chicago and London: University of Chicago Press

UK Government (1999) *Convention on the Rights of the Child: Second report to the UN Committee on the Rights of the Child by the United Kingdom*, London: HMSO

United Nations (1985) United Nations Standard Minimum Rules for the Administration of Juvenile Justice: Beijing Rules: Resolution 40/33

United Nations (1989) *United Nations Convention of the Rights of the Child: Resolution 44/25*. Available at URL: www2.ohchr.org/english/law/crc.htm

United Nations (1990) United Nations Guidelines for the Prevention of Juvenile Delinquency: Riyadh Guidelines: Resolution 45/112

United Nations (1990), *United Nations Rules for the Protection of Juveniles Deprived of their Liberty: Resolution 45/113*

United Nations Committee on the Rights of the Child (2002) *Consideration of Reports Submitted by State Parties under Article 44 of the Convention, CRC/15/Add.188, 9 October*

Utting, D. and Vennard, J. (2000) *What Works with Young Offenders in the Community?* Ilford: Barnardo's

Waiton, S. (2008) *The Politics of Antisocial Behaviour: Amoral Panics*, London: Routledge

Walker, M., Barclay, A., Hunter, L., Kendrick, A., Malloch, M., Hill, M. And McIvor, G. (2005*) Secure Accommodation in Scotland: Its Role and Relationship with Alternative Services: Report of Research for the Scottish Executive Education Department*, Edinburgh: Scottish Executive

Walklate, S. (2001) 'Community and crime prevention' in Muncie, J. and McLaughlin, E. (eds) (2001) *Controlling Crime*, London: Sage

Walters, R. and Woodward, R. (2007) 'Punishing "poor parents": "respect", "responsibility" and Parenting Orders in Scotland', *Youth Justice*, Vol. 7, No. 5, pp. 5–20

Waterhouse, L. and McGhee, J. (2000) *The Evaluation of Children's Hearings in Scotland. Volume 3: Children in Focus*, Edinburgh: Scottish Executive

Waterhouse, L. and McGhee, J. (2002) 'Children's Hearings in Scotland: compulsion and disadvantage', *Journal of Social Welfare and Family Law*, Vol. 24, No. 3, pp. 279–96

Waterhouse, L. McGhee, J. and Whyte, B. (2002) 'Children's Hearings and children in trouble', in Muncie, J., Hughes G. and McLaughlin, E. (eds) (2002) *Youth Justice: Critical Readings*, London: Sage

Waterhouse, L., McGhee, J. and Loucks, N. (2004) 'Disentangling offenders and non-offenders in the Scottish Children's Hearings: a clear divide?' *Howard Journal of Criminal Justice*, Vol. 43, No. 2, pp. 164–79

Waterhouse, L., McGhee, J., Whyte, B., Loucks, N., Kay, H. and Stewart, R. (2000) *Evaluation of Children's Hearings in Scotland, Volume 3: Children in Focus*, Edinburgh: Scottish Executive

Whyte, B. (2000a) 'Between two stools: youth justice in Scotland', *Probation Journal*, Vol. 47, No. 2, pp. 119–25

Whyte, B. (2000b) 'Youth justice in Scotland', in Pickford, J. (ed.) (2000) *Youth Justice in Theory and Practice*, London: Cavendish

Whyte, B. (2003) 'Young and persistent: recent developments in youth justice policy and practice in Scotland', *Youth Justice*, Vol. 3, No. 2, pp. 74–85

Whyte, B. (2004) 'Responding to youth crime in Scotland', *British Journal of Social Work*, Vol. 34, pp. 395–411

Whyte, B. (2005) 'Youth justice in other UK jurisdictions: Scotland and Northern Ireland', in Bateman, T. and Pitts, J. (eds) (2005) *The RHP Companion to Youth Justice*, Lyme Regis: Russell House Publishing

Whyte, B. (2006) 'Change, evidence, challenges: youth justice developments in Scotland', in Hill, M., Lockyer, A. and Stone, F. (eds) (2006) *Youth Justice and Child Protection*, London: Jessica Kingsley

Whyte, B. (2007) 'Youth justice: developments in Scotland for the 21st century', in McIvor, G. and Raynor, P. (eds) (2007) *Developments in Social Work with Offenders. Research Highlights*, London: Jessica Kingsley

Whyte, B. (2009) COUNTERBLAST: 'Youth "In Justice" in the UK – Which Way for Scotland?', *Howard Journal of Criminal Justice*, Vol. 48, No. 2, pp. 200–4

Williams, B. (2005) *Victims of Crime and Community Justice*, London: Jessica Kingsley

Wilson, J. Q. and Kelling, G. (1982) 'Broken windows: the police and neighbourhood safety, *Atlantic Monthly*, March, pp. 29–38

Young, J. (1999) *The Exclusive Society: Social Exclusion, Crime and Difference in Late Modernity*, London, Sage

Youth Court Feasibility Project Group (2002) *Youth Court Feasibility Group Report*, Justice Department, Edinburgh: Scottish Executive

Youth Justice Board, *Youth Justice Annual Statistics 2003/2004 (B193)*

Index